Date: 7/26/12

795.4153 IZD
Izdebski, Wladyslaw.
Deadly defence /

DEADLY DEFF

For well over for_____ *fence at*
Bridge has been _____ defence.
Now a serious challenge is being _____ markable
new book to take the game forward in the twenty-first century.
Deadly Defence covers every important aspect to make good
players into excellent defenders. It deals with opening leads
(how to convey maximum information), defensive play when
playing second hand, third hand and also when you are first to
play to a trick, how to use signals more effectively and how to
think on defence like an expert.

*Wladyslaw Izdebski is a certified bridge teacher and the
author of over twenty books and hundreds of articles on
bridge theory. He is the former chief editor of the monthly
'Swiat Brydza' (The World of Bridge).*

*Roman Krzemien is a certified bridge teacher and the author
of four books on bridge and hundreds of articles in bridge
and non-bridge journals. For many years he has trained and
captained the Polish National Women's Team.*

*Ron Klinger is a leading international bridge teacher and
author. He has written over fifty books, some of which have
been translated into Bulgarian, Chinese, Danish, French,
Hebrew and Icelandic. He has also represented Australia
in many world championships and international tournaments
from 1976 to 2010. He won the BOLS Brilliancy Prize for his
defence on a deal during the 1976 World Teams Olympiad.*

PALM BEACH COUNTY
LIBRARY SYSTEM
3650 SUMMIT BLVD.
WEST PALM BEACH, FL 33406

By RON KLINGER *in the Master Bridge Series*

BASIC BRIDGE: *The Guide to Good Acol Bidding and Play*
BETTER BRIDGE WITH A BETTER MEMORY • BRIDGE IS FUN
THE POWER OF SHAPE • WHEN TO BID, WHEN TO PASS
*GUIDE TO BETTER CARD PLAY • PLAYING TO WIN AT BRIDGE
GUIDE TO BETTER ACOL BRIDGE • 20 GREAT CONVENTIONS FLIPPER
GUIDE TO BETTER DUPLICATE BRIDGE • CUE-BIDDING TO SLAMS
BRIDGE CONVENTIONS, DEFENCES AND COUNTERMEASURES
100 WINNING BRIDGE TIPS • 50 MORE WINNING BRIDGE TIPS
100 WINNING DUPLICATE TIPS • ACOL BRIDGE MADE EASY
THE MODERN LOSING TRICK COUNT • PRACTICAL SLAM BIDDING
IMPROVE YOUR BRIDGE MEMORY • IMPROVE YOUR DECLARER PLAY AT NO-TRUMPS
IMPROVE YOUR OPENING LEADS • ACOL BRIDGE FLIPPER
RON KLINGER'S MASTER CLASS • 5-CARD MAJOR STAYMAN
RON KLINGER ANSWERS YOUR BRIDGE QUERIES
THE LAW OF TOTAL TRICKS FLIPPER • BASIC ACOL BRIDGE FLIPPER
DUPLICATE BRIDGE FLIPPER • MODERN LOSING TRICK COUNT FLIPPER
MEMORY AIDS & USEFUL RULES FLIPPER
BID BETTER, MUCH BETTER AFTER OPENING 1 NO-TRUMP
5-CARD MAJORS • 5-CARD MAJORS FLIPPER
TO WIN AT BRIDGE • †RIGHT THROUGH THE PACK AGAIN

*Winner of the 1991 Book of the Year Award of the American Bridge Teachers' Association
†Winner of the 2009 International Bridge Association Book of the Year Award

with David Bird
KOSHER BRIDGE
THE RABBI'S MAGIC TRICK: *More Kosher Bridge*

with Andrew Kambites
UNDERSTANDING THE CONTESTED AUCTION
UNDERSTANDING THE UNCONTESTED AUCTION
UNDERSTANDING SLAM BIDDING
UNDERSTANDING DUPLICATE PAIRS
HOW GOOD IS YOUR BRIDGE HAND?
BRIDGE CONVENTIONS FOR YOU
CARD PLAY MADE EASY 2: *Know Your Suit Combinations*
CARD PLAY MADE EASY 3: *Trump Management*

with Hugh Kelsey
NEW INSTANT GUIDE TO BRIDGE

with Mike Lawrence
OPENING LEADS FOR ACOL PLAYERS
OPENING LEADS FLIPPER

with Derek Rimington
IMPROVE YOUR BIDDING AND PLAY

with David Jackson
BETTER BALANCED BIDDING

DEADLY
DEFENCE

by
Wladyslaw Izdebski,
Roman Krzemien
and
Ron Klinger

Weidenfeld & Nicolson
IN ASSOCIATION WITH
PETER CRAWLEY

First published in Great Britain 2011
Second impression 2011
in association with Peter Crawley
by Weidenfeld & Nicolson
a division of the Orion Publishing Group Ltd
Orion House, 5 Upper St Martin's Lane, London, WC2H 9EA

an Hachette UK Company

© Wladyslaw Izdebski, Roman Krzemien and Ron Klinger 2011

All rights reserved. No part of this publication may be reproduced, stored in
a retrieval system, or transmitted, in any form or by any means, electronic,
mechanical, photocopying, recording or otherwise, without the prior permission
of both the copyright owners and the above publisher.

The right of Wladyslaw Izdebski, Roman Krzemien and Ron Klinger to be
identified as the authors of this book has been asserted by them in accordance
with the Copyright, Designs and Patents Act 1988.

A catalogue record for this book is available from the British Library

ISBN: 978 0 297 86350 2

Typeset by Modern Bridge Publications
P.O. Box 140, Northbridge NSW 1560, Australia

Printed in Great Britain by Clays Ltd, St Ives plc

The Orion Publishing Group's policy is to use papers that are natural, renewable
and recyclable products and made from wood grown in sustainable forests.
The logging and manufacturing processes are expected to conform to the
environmental regulations of the country of origin.

www.orionbooks.co.uk

Acknowledgement

This English version of *Deadly Defence* would not have been possible without
the excellent translation from the original Polish by Wally Malaczynski and
his assistants, Andrew Adamczewski, Peter Ciszak, George Czubala, Richard
Waszyrowski and Jack Wociac.

Contents

Introduction

Dear bridge player,

Without a doubt, defence is the hardest part of bridge. Every average player knows the principles of bidding and sensible ways to play as declarer, but when it comes to defence, players make mistake after mistake. This is often the result of insufficient information to make the right choice.

Whether it is the opening lead or later defence, players might not know enough about partner's hand, yet this can be the most important element in making the correct decision.

This book takes you through the elements of sound opening leads, winning actions in second seat and third seat, the right card to lead in the mid-game, the best use of attitude signals, count signals and suit-preference signals, how to false-card effectively, and much, much more. It also shows you how to soar above slavish adherence to rules. You will marvel at how defenders can defeat seemingly impregnable contacts by creating illusions in the mind of declarer.

Everything is aimed at improving your partnership's level of defence and to instil good habits into you and your partner. Another object is to try to make certain defensive plays automatic, so that you do not have to invest a great deal of thought when they occur.

And so, let's start and you can look forward to guaranteed improved results at the table.

Wladyslaw Izdebski, Roman Krzemien, 2010

Prologue
How to defeat cold contracts

This is not about defence against a beginner, who can misplay any hand, but about defending against a competent declarer. Consider this deal:

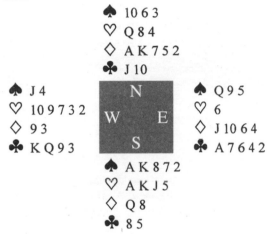

```
              ♠ 10 6 3
              ♡ Q 8 4
              ◇ A K 7 5 2
              ♣ J 10
  ♠ J 4          N          ♠ Q 9 5
  ♡ 10 9 7 3 2              ♡ 6
  ◇ 9 3     W       E       ◇ J 10 6 4
  ♣ K Q 9 3       S         ♣ A 7 6 4 2
              ♠ A K 8 7 2
              ♡ A K J 5
              ◇ Q 8
              ♣ 8 5
```

South is in 4♠ and you will rarely find a colder contract. There are just three obvious losers, two clubs and a spade. Can you see any way that declarer might go down while following a rational line of play?

Let's take a look. West leads the ♣K, followed by the ♣3 to the ♣A. East switches to the ♡6. South wins and cashes the ♠A. On this East plays the ♠Q! If South now cashes the ♠K, there will be two trump losers if West began with ♠J-9-5-4.

To cater for that, South plays a low spade from hand. West wins with the ♠J and returns a heart for East to ruff. One down!

For this brilliant defence, Primo Levi, East, won the Best Defence of
the Year Award in 1988 from the International Bridge Press
Association. Twenty years earlier the famous Swiss player, Jean
Besse, produced the identical brilliancy on this deal:

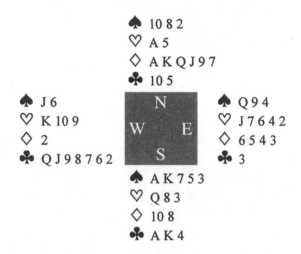

```
                       ♠ 10 8 2
                       ♡ A 5
                       ◇ A K Q J 9 7
                       ♣ 10 5
    ♠ J 6                  N              ♠ Q 9 4
    ♡ K 10 9                              ♡ J 7 6 4 2
    ◇ 2           W              E        ◇ 6 5 4 3
    ♣ Q J 9 8 7 6 2          S            ♣ 3
                       ♠ A K 7 5 3
                       ♡ Q 8 3
                       ◇ 10 8
                       ♣ A K 4
```

South is in 6♠ on the lead of the ♣Q. Again the contract looks
routine. Cash the top spades and claim, discarding the heart and
the club losers on dummy's diamonds.

From the lead East knew that South had the ♣A, ♣K. With that
solid diamond suit in dummy, East could tell there would be one
trump trick at best for the defence and so the only hope was a
little subterfuge. The most it would cost would be an overtrick.

South won trick 1 and played the ♠A. East calmly dropped the
♠Q. South naturally continued with a low spade. West won and
played another club. East ruffed and another cold contract had
bitten the dust.

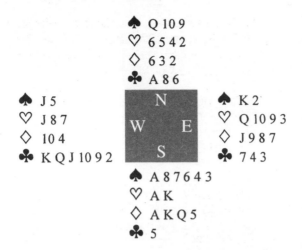

♠ Q 10 9
♡ 6 5 4 2
◇ 6 3 2
♣ A 8 6

♠ J 5
♡ J 8 7
◇ 10 4
♣ K Q J 10 9 2

♠ K 2
♡ Q 10 9 3
◇ J 9 8 7
♣ 7 4 3

♠ A 8 7 6 4 3
♡ A K
◇ A K Q 5
♣ 5

West opened 3♣ and South ended in 6♠. With spades 2-2, declarer can play trumps and later ruff the fourth diamond in dummy. Can you see any way that the defenders might prevail?

Looks impossible? Not when West is Zia Mahmood, formerly of Pakistan, now in the USA, and one of the world's best players. Look what happened: West led the ♣K, taken in dummy, and declarer played a low spade to the ace. West dropped the ♠J.

You can see declarer's reasoning. Another spade could be fatal if East began with ♠K-5-2. East would win and play a third spade. Now if the diamonds are not 3-3, declarer has another loser.

South saw a solution. If the diamonds were not 3-3, then, given the 3♣ opening, West figured to be the one short in diamonds, not East. If East started with 4+ diamonds, playing to ruff a diamond first looked to be safe, as West was out of trumps.

South played ◇A, ◇K, ◇Q. West ruffed with the low spade and South was one down. Of course, South should play the ♠Q from dummy at trick 2, as the ♠K is almost certainly with East. Still, that is not your problem as a defender.

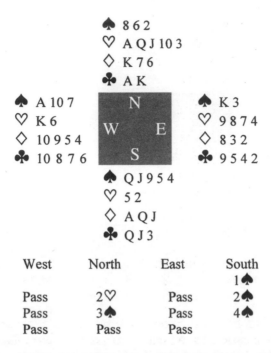

West	North	East	South
			1♠
Pass	2♡	Pass	2♠
Pass	3♠	Pass	4♠
Pass	Pass	Pass	

On any normal day declarer would make eleven tricks, losing only to the top trump honours. With Andrew Zurek of Poland in the West seat, it was not a normal day. In a teams event in Milan, he managed to defeat 4♠. Can you see how that could happen?

West led the ♡6. Fearing this to be a singleton, declarer rose with dummy's ♡A. He continued with a low spade to the jack and ace. West cashed the ♡K and played a diamond in the hope of finding East with the ◇A. East lacked that card, but had one just as good.

Declarer won in dummy and led a second spade. East won with the ♠K and played a third round of hearts. South was void in hearts, but so was West. The third heart promoted West's ♠10 for the fourth trick for the defence.

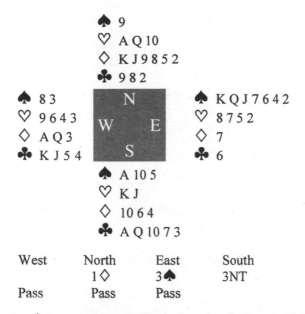

West	North	East	South
	1◇	3♠	3NT
Pass	Pass	Pass	

With the ◇A-Q onside, this looked to be declarer's lucky day. Eleven tricks seemed assured. With Maurice Harrison-Gray in the West seat, South's day took a decidedly unlucky turn.

Take a look at Harrison-Gray's defence. West led the ♠8 and declarer ducked East's ♠J and ♠K. South took the third spade and West discarded . . . the ace of diamonds!

Fearing that East now had an entry with the ◇Q, South decided to focus on the club suit. The ♡J to dummy's ♡Q was followed by the ♣9, which ran to West's ♣J. Harrison-Gray shifted to the ◇3.

With no intention of departing from his line of play, South won with dummy's ◇K. When he played another club, there was no way to avoid going one down. The defence came to two spades, one diamond and two clubs. Just as well that South did not take the second spade, otherwise West's brilliancy would have never come to light.

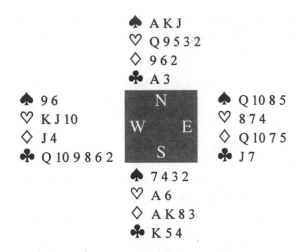

```
              ♠ A K J
              ♡ Q 9 5 3 2
              ◇ 9 6 2
              ♣ A 3
♠ 9 6                        ♠ Q 10 8 5
♡ K J 10          N         ♡ 8 7 4
◇ J 4         W       E     ◇ Q 10 7 5
♣ Q 10 9 8 6 2    S         ♣ J 7
              ♠ 7 4 3 2
              ♡ A 6
              ◇ A K 8 3
              ♣ K 5 4
```

South is in 3NT on the ♣10 lead. South takes the ♣A, and plays a low heart to the ace. West drops the ♡K. Thinking hearts are 5-1, South switches to spades and that leads to the defeat of 3NT.

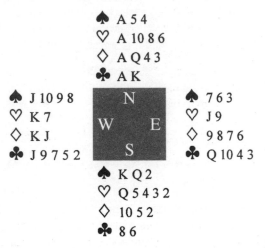

```
              ♠ A 5 4
              ♡ A 10 8 6
              ◇ A Q 4 3
              ♣ A K
♠ J 10 9 8                  ♠ 7 6 3
♡ K 7            N          ♡ J 9
◇ K J        W       E      ◇ 9 8 7 6
♣ J 9 7 5 2      S          ♣ Q 10 4 3
              ♠ K Q 2
              ♡ Q 5 4 3 2
              ◇ 10 5 2
              ♣ 8 6
```

South is in 6♡ on the ♠J lead. How would you plan the play?

Unaware that the miraculous position meant there was no loser in diamonds, South aimed to avoid losing a trick in trumps. That was possible only if the trump layout looked like this:

♡ A 10 8 6

♡ K 9 7   ♡ J

♡ Q 5 4 3 2

Playing for precisely this, declarer took the spade lead with the king and led the ♡Q: king – ace – jack! Happy with the outcome, South came to hand with the ♠Q and finessed the ♡8. Surprise! East won with the ♡9 and now the contract had to go one down. South had no entry to hand to take a winning finesse in diamonds.

This deal has a similar theme:

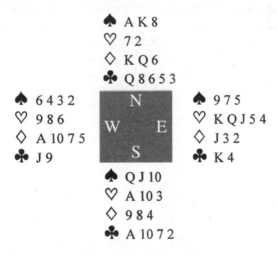

♠ A K 8
♡ 7 2
◊ K Q 6
♣ Q 8 6 5 3

♠ 6 4 3 2   ♠ 9 7 5
♡ 9 8 6   ♡ K Q J 5 4
◊ A 10 7 5   ◊ J 3 2
♣ J 9   ♣ K 4

♠ Q J 10
♡ A 10 3
◊ 9 8 4
♣ A 10 7 2

The deal arose in the 1990 Sunday Times Cup, in which 16 pairs competed, by invitation only. At every table South played 3NT on a heart lead, ducked twice. After taking the third heart three Souths played a spade to dummy, followed by a low club to the ten. With clubs 2-2 and the ◊A with West, 3NT was home.

At the fourth table the declarer was Jim Jacoby, USA. He saw a chance of making 3NT which did not depend on the location of the ♦A. To achieve that he needed to score five club tricks. That required the club layout to look like this:

♣ Q 8 6 5 3

♣ J   ♣ K 9 4

♣ A 10 7 2

Declarer crossed to dummy with a spade and played the ♣Q. East covered with the king and when South played the ♣A, West followed with the ♣J!

South's dream split had come true. He crossed to dummy with another spade and took the 'marked' finesse against East's ♣9.
To South's amazement, West won the trick and played a third round of spades. This set up the fourth spade as a winner with the ♦A as the entry. That gave the defence five tricks and to make matters worse, West was Bobby Goldman, a friend of Jacoby's and also a member of the famous Dallas Aces team.

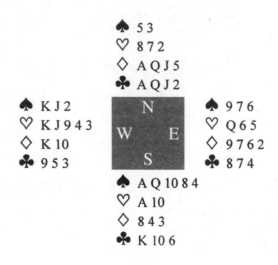

♠ 5 3
♡ 8 7 2
♦ A Q J 5
♣ A Q J 2

♠ K J 2
♡ K J 9 4 3
♦ K 10
♣ 9 5 3

♠ 9 7 6
♡ Q 6 5
♦ 9 7 6 2
♣ 8 7 4

♠ A Q 10 8 4
♡ A 10
♦ 8 4 3
♣ K 10 6

South was in 3NT on the ♡4 lead. He felt his best chance for success was the diamond finesse rather than the double finesse in spades. After some thought South decided that he could improve his chances. Perhaps West had the ♠K singleton. If so, he would not need the diamond finesse. Accordingly he cashed the ♠A and West dropped the ♠K!

Pleased with his analysis South crossed to dummy in clubs and finessed the ♠8. West won and cashed his hearts for one down.

Take a look at this defence by Michael Lawrence, Dallas Aces:

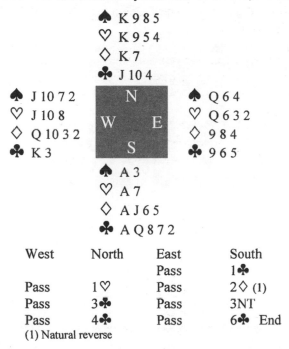

```
                    ♠ K 9 8 5
                    ♡ K 9 5 4
                    ◇ K 7
                    ♣ J 10 4
   ♠ J 10 7 2        N          ♠ Q 6 4
   ♡ J 10 8      W       E      ♡ Q 6 3 2
   ◇ Q 10 3 2                   ◇ 9 8 4
   ♣ K 3             S          ♣ 9 6 5
                    ♠ A 3
                    ♡ A 7
                    ◇ A J 6 5
                    ♣ A Q 8 7 2
```

West	North	East	South
		Pass	1♣
Pass	1♡	Pass	2◇ (1)
Pass	3♣	Pass	3NT
Pass	4♣	Pass	6♣ End

(1) Natural reverse

West led the ♠J. South won and played ◇K, diamond to the ace and ruffed the third diamond. Lawrence felt South was bound to have the four aces plus the ♣Q and a 2-2-4-5 or a 3-1-5-4 pattern, since he had bid 3NT over 3♣.

If West had followed low on the three diamonds, South would ruff the fourth diamond and lose only to the ♣K. Therefore Lawrence played the ◇Q on the third round of diamonds. That was not yet enough to complete a fine defence. Declarer led the ♣J from dummy, playing low from hand. Lawrence followed low! Declarer continued with the ♣10 to repeat the club finesse. Now Lawrence took the ♣K and gave East a diamond ruff.

And now a cold grand slam . . . but not so cold after all:

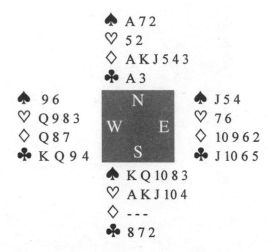

                    ♠ A 7 2
                    ♡ 5 2
                    ◇ A K J 5 4 3
                    ♣ A 3

 ♠ 9 6   ♠ J 5 4
 ♡ Q 9 8 3   ♡ 7 6
 ◇ Q 8 7   ◇ 10 9 6 2
 ♣ K Q 9 4   ♣ J 10 6 5

                    ♠ K Q 10 8 3
                    ♡ A K J 10 4
                    ◇ - - -
                    ♣ 8 7 2

South was in 7♠ on the lead of the ♣K. The best hope looked to be to cash the ◇A, ◇K and ruff a diamond. If the ◇Q fell, South would have three discards after drawing trumps, ending in dummy.

South played two rounds of spades and then cashed the ◇A and ◇K. West played the ◇Q on the second round! To declarer this meant that East began with five diamonds. If so, the diamonds could not be established for three discards.

South switched plans and played ♡A, ♡K, followed by the ♡J.
West played low and South ruffed the third heart in dummy. East
over-ruffed and South still had to lose to the ♡Q. Two down.

Next, take a look at Zia Mahmood in action as East on this deal:

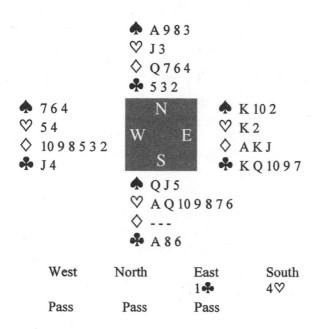

```
              ♠ A 9 8 3
              ♡ J 3
              ◇ Q 7 6 4
              ♣ 5 3 2
♠ 7 6 4              N          ♠ K 10 2
♡ 5 4                           ♡ K 2
◇ 10 9 8 5 3 2   W    E         ◇ A K J
♣ J 4                S          ♣ K Q 10 9 7
              ♠ Q J 5
              ♡ A Q 10 9 8 7 6
              ◇ - - -
              ♣ A 8 6
```

West	North	East	South
		1♣	4♡
Pass	Pass	Pass	

South played 4♡ on the ♣J lead. South won with the ♣A and led
the ♠Q. Everyone followed low, East playing the ♠10! Figuring
that there was no spade loser any more South continued with the
♡A and a second heart.

That was just what Zia had hoped. He took the ♡K, cashed two
clubs and still collected the ♠K later.

On the next deal, from the 1988 World Teams Olympiad, a safety play in trumps turned out to be not so safe after all:

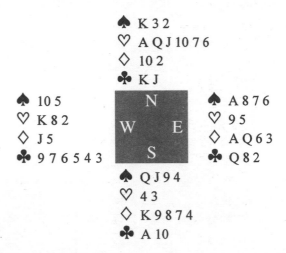

♠ K 3 2
♥ A Q J 10 7 6
♦ 10 2
♣ K J

♠ 10 5
♥ K 8 2
♦ J 5
♣ 9 7 6 5 4 3

♠ A 8 7 6
♥ 9 5
♦ A Q 6 3
♣ Q 8 2

♠ Q J 9 4
♥ 4 3
♦ K 9 8 7 4
♣ A 10

South was in 4♥ against one of the best pairs in the world, Jeff Meckstroth and Eric Rodwell. West led the ♦J and Rodwell, East, took the ♦A and switched to the ♠8.

Anxious to avoid East scoring a spade ruff, South played the hearts from the top: ♥A and then the ♥Q. West took the ♥K, played a spade to East's ace and West was the one who had the spade ruff.

Here is world champion Maurice Aujaleu in action:

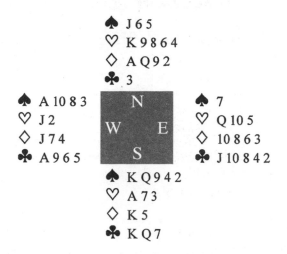

♠ J 6 5
♡ K 9 8 6 4
◇ A Q 9 2
♣ 3

♠ A 10 8 3
♡ J 2
◇ J 7 4
♣ A 9 6 5

♠ 7
♡ Q 10 5
◇ 10 8 6 3
♣ J 10 8 4 2

♠ K Q 9 4 2
♡ A 7 3
◇ K 5
♣ K Q 7

South was in 4♡, which can be beaten easily via the ♠A, spade ruff, club to the ace, spade ruff, but West led the ♡J. Now 4♡ is cold, but not against Aujaleu. Declarer played low in dummy and Aujaleu followed with the ♡Q! South took the ♡A and finessed the ♡9. East won and shifted to the ♠7. He scored his spade ruff and the ♣A meant one down.

Now that you are aware how beautifully champions can defend, you will want to bring your own defence to the same level. Please move on to the next chapter. While we cannot guarantee that you will become as great as these defenders, you will not be wasting your time and your defence is bound to improve.

Chapter 1
Leads and signalling methods

In the last few decades, top players have experimented with many different approaches for opening leads and signals. Many have focussed on improving bidding methods, with new conventions, new gadgets, new styles, and the gains from these can be clearly seen. With a new approach to opening leads, the improvement is not so easy to discern. In bidding there is a constant stream of new ideas, which are tested and then adopted or discarded. When it comes to opening leads, however, new ideas occur only rarely.

In declarer play, there are almost no new discoveries. When it comes to leads, signals and defensive technique, this book is most comprehensive. Your system for leads is important, but not as important as your signalling and defensive understandings with your partner(s). These are the areas that need to be most effective.

Our System of Leads: This system for opening leads has become the most popular approach in Poland:

Table of opening leads

From low card holdings:

x-<u>x</u>   Lead the bottom card from a doubleton
x-<u>x</u>-x   Lead middle – down – up from three worthless cards
x-<u>x</u>-x-x   Lead second-highest. Follow with the top card next time, as long as you can afford this, to show an even number.

From honour card holdings:

<u>H</u>-x   Lead top
H-<u>x</u>-x   Lead second-highest
H-x-x-<u>x</u>   Lead bottom
H-x-x-<u>x</u>(-x)   Fourth-best

If you do not fancy this system for opening leads, by all means retain the approach with which you are happy and familiar, such as fourth-highest, or thirds-and-fifths, or middle-up-down. You will see in the many example deals that it is rarely the specific card led that is critical, but what follows. However, for leads from honour sequences, we do strongly recommend the following:

Leads from specific honour holdings:

A from A-K-x
K from K-Q-x or A-K bare
Q from Q-J-x, or in no-trumps, from A-Q-J-x(-x)
J from J-10-x or K-J-10-x or, in no-trumps, from A-J-10-x(-x)
10 from 10-x, K-10-9-x, Q-10-9-x or, in no-trumps, A-10-9-x(-x)

Signalling

High-low to show an even number and high-encouraging are known as 'standard signals', but strongly recommended and greatly preferred by most top players are reverse signals:

Count signals

Low-high = an even number of cards
High-low = an odd number of cards

This is the opposite of natural count signals and is known as reverse count.

Attitude signals

Lowest and low-high = encouraging
Highest or high-low = discouraging

This is the opposite of natural attitude signals and is known as reverse attitude. Let's take a look at some deals which show that reverse signals are superior and help partner make the right decision.

(A)
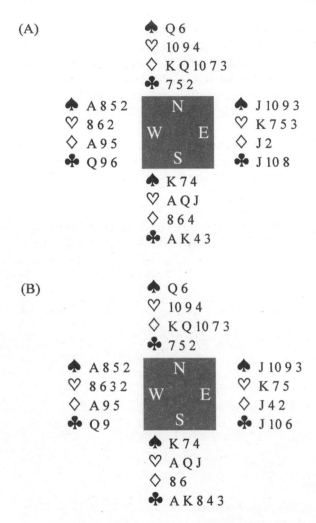

(B)

For both these deals South is in 3NT after 1NT : 2NT, 3NT. West starts with the ♠2. Declarer plays the ♠Q from dummy and East follows with the ♠J to show the sequence. South takes the heart finesse and leads a diamond to dummy's ◇K.

If you use natural signals, East has to play the ◇2 in each case. To play the ◇J with a doubleton would remove any guess for declarer on the second round. It might be vital to leave declarer with a guess in diamonds if South had a hand like this:

♠ K 7 4   ♡ A Q 2   ◇ 8 6 4   ♣ A K Q 3

In this case South needs to score two diamond tricks to make 3NT. If East drops the ◇J, natural signals, the hand is over. Only by playing low can East give declarer a guess on the second round of diamonds.

After winning with the ◇K, declarer repeats the heart finesse and leads another diamond. In (A) West must play low to defeat the contract, while in (B), West must take the ◇A on the second round.

If you play reverse count, East (A) plays the ◇2 on the first round to show an even number. West then knows to duck the second round. This cannot hurt the defence, whether South has three or four diamonds.

East (B) should drop the ◇J under the ◇K on the first round of diamonds. This does no damage if West began with ◇A-x and makes it clear to West with ◇A-x-x that East started with three diamonds and hence South has only a doubleton. With ◇J-x-x, you cannot afford to play the middle card, since that would be ambiguous to West. It could be bottom from J-x.

Note that the reverse count signals enlighten West in both cases, while West is left to guess if East-West play natural signals.

West dealer : Nil vulnerable

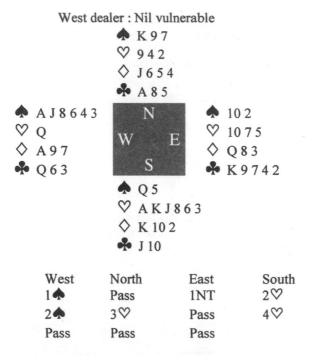

```
                    ♠ K 9 7
                    ♡ 9 4 2
                    ◊ J 6 5 4
                    ♣ A 8 5
♠ A J 8 6 4 3                        ♠ 10 2
♡ Q              N                   ♡ 10 7 5
◊ A 9 7      W       E               ◊ Q 8 3
♣ Q 6 3          S                   ♣ K 9 7 4 2
                    ♠ Q 5
                    ♡ A K J 8 6 3
                    ◊ K 10 2
                    ♣ J 10
```

West	North	East	South
1♠	Pass	1NT	2♡
2♠	3♡	Pass	4♡
Pass	Pass	Pass	

West leads the ♠A. If East plays the ♠10, natural signals, high-encourage, South has an easy time. South drops the ♠Q and can finesse the ♠9 later for a club discard.

When East plays the ♠2, reverse signals, South has no benefit by dropping the ♠Q. West shifts to a club and now South cannot make the contract. Dummy has no entry to reach the ♠K later and South will lose one spade, one club and two diamonds.

These have been good examples of the benefits of playing reverse count when holding honour doubleton, such as J-x or 10-x. With natural signals, you do not want to squander the honour, but when you do not, you might give partner a misleading message or give declarer a chance to make the contract.

It can also happen that playing a low card as a natural signal might be a disaster. Take a look at this deal:

South dealer : Both vulnerable

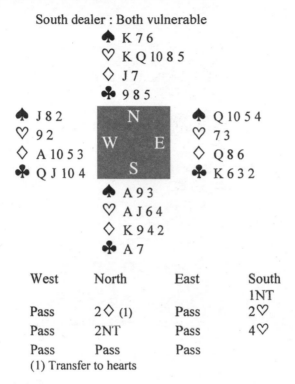

♠ K 7 6
♡ K Q 10 8 5
◇ J 7
♣ 9 8 5

♠ J 8 2
♡ 9 2
◇ A 10 5 3
♣ Q J 10 4

♠ Q 10 5 4
♡ 7 3
◇ Q 8 6
♣ K 6 3 2

♠ A 9 3
♡ A J 6 4
◇ K 9 4 2
♣ A 7

West	North	East	South
			1NT
Pass	2◇ (1)	Pass	2♡
Pass	2NT	Pass	4♡
Pass	Pass	Pass	

(1) Transfer to hearts

West leads the ♣Q. South wins and plays the ◇2. Suppose West follows with the ◇5, natural count. Dummy's ◇J is taken by the ◇Q and the defenders continue with two rounds of clubs. South ruffs the third club and draws trumps with the ♡A and a heart to the king.

Now declarer plays the ◇7 from dummy: eight – nine – ten. West exits with a low spade to the queen and ace. As East did not rise with the ◇A when the ◇7 was led from dummy, South can reasonably place the ◇A with West. South continues with the ◇K.

If West ducks, South discards a spade from dummy. If West takes
the ◇K with the ◇A, South's ◇4 has become the top diamond,
again allowing a spade discard.

Notice this cannot happen if you are playing reverse count. On the
◇2 from South, West follows with the ◇3, lowest from an even
number. Now South's ◇4 cannot become a winner.

Now let's see how reverse signals can be helpful when you give
encouraging or discouraging signals:

South dealer : Both vulnerable

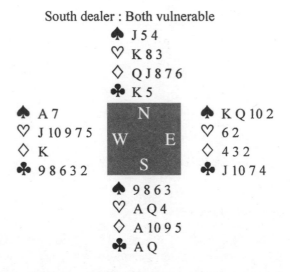

♠ J 5 4
♡ K 8 3
◇ Q J 8 7 6
♣ K 5

♠ A 7   ♠ K Q 10 2
♡ J 10 9 7 5   ♡ 6 2
◇ K   ◇ 4 3 2
♣ 9 8 6 3 2   ♣ J 10 7 4

♠ 9 8 6 3
♡ A Q 4
◇ A 10 9 5
♣ A Q

After 1NT from South, raised to 3NT by North, West leads the
♡J. Declarer wins in dummy and leads the ◇Q, letting it run
when East plays low. West wins with the ◇K and, with no future
in hearts, shifts to a black suit. A spade will work on the actual
deal, but a club would be necessary if East began with ♣A-Q-x-x.

To retain both options, West tries the ♠A first. Playing natural signals, if East encourages with the ♠10, that is fatal. South now loses only three spade tricks. On the other hand if East follows with the ♠2, low discouraging, West will abandon spades and hope to beat 3NT with a club shift.

Playing reverse signals, East plays the ♠2, low encouraging, on the ♠A. The next spade gives the defence three more tricks to take 3NT one down.

Suppose the bidding has been:

West	North	East	South
			1♣
Pass	1♡	Pass	1NT
Pass	Pass	Pass	

The spade layout might be like this:

(a)
```
                ♠ A 8 5
   ♠ K Q 10 6              ♠ J 4 2
                ♠ 9 7 3
```

(b)
```
                ♠ A 8 5
   ♠ K Q 10 6              ♠ 9 4 2
                ♠ J 7 3
```

In each case West leads the ♠K and declarer plays low from dummy. If East plays the ♠4 as a come-on in (a), natural signals, West cannot tell who has the jack. When declarer follows with the ♠3, West will not know whether East began with J-4-2 or 9-7-4.

Note South's ♠3, which is the right play. If South plays the ♠7, West would have little problem placing the jack with East.

Remember: When you are declarer, you need to know the opponents' signalling methods and do exactly the same yourself. If the opponents play natural signals, then if you as declarer do not want the suit continued, you should play low-discouraging. If the opponents play reverse signals and you want a suit continued, you should play lowest as declarer. If you do not want a defender to continue a suit, follow with as high a card as you can afford. Perhaps this will create some doubt in the defender's mind whether partner's card was high or low.

Reverting to the previous example: If playing reverse signals, West has no trouble. In (a) East plays the ♠2, lowest to encourage and hence East must have the jack. In (b) East plays the ♠9, high to discourage. Now West places the ♠J with South and shifts to another suit.

It is conceivable that natural signals do work better in some cases, but these are very rare instances. Statistically, low-encourage, high-discourage will come out best most of the time.

Chapter 2
Attitude signals,
Encourage – Discourage

In bidding, many sequences are available and so there is great scope for imparting important information to partner. With signals, the range of information is much smaller. When defending, the vital message is how the defence should proceed to best effect. This is far more important than telling partner how many cards you have in the suit played or whether you hold an honour card in that suit or not.

To prove this point, consider this deal:

Dealer West : Nil vulnerable

NORTH
♠ A 7 6
♡ 10 8 6 3
♢ Q 10 5 2
♣ A K

WEST
♠ Q J 10 8 3
♡ A 7
♢ A 6 3
♣ 10 8 4

EAST
♠ K 9 5 2
♡ 5 4
♢ K 7
♣ J 6 5 3 2

SOUTH
♠ 4
♡ K Q J 9 2
♢ J 9 8 4
♣ Q 9 7

West	North	East	South
Pass	1♢	Pass	1♡
1♠	2♡	2♠	4♡
Pass	Pass	Pass	

West leads the ♠Q, taken by the ace. South plays a heart to the king and ace. To defeat 4♡, West now must play a low diamond. East wins with the ♢K, returns a diamond to the ace and ruffs the third diamond. On any other defence 4♡ makes easily.

At trick 1, as East can see that the only hope for the defence is for West to have the ♢A, East plays the ♠9 under the ♠A to discourage a spade continuation. West should now find the winning defence.

However, what if the deal looked like this? Again West leads the
♠Q against 4♡. South wins and plays a heart . . .

Dealer West : Nil vulnerable

                    ♠ A 7 6
                    ♡ 10 8 6 3
                    ◊ Q 10 5 2
                    ♣ A K

♠ Q J 10 8 3   ♠ K 9 5 2
♡ A 7   ♡ 5 4
◊ A 6 3   ◊ J 7
♣ 10 8 4   ♣ J 6 5 3 2

                    ♠ 4
                    ♡ K Q J 9 2
                    ◊ K 9 8 4
                    ♣ Q 9 7

If West wins the ♡A and shifts to a diamond, South makes easily.
West's diamond lead has solved any guess in diamonds. Here
West needs to exit with a spade. Now South has to tackle
diamonds himself and might lose two diamond tricks.

Here East does not want West to shift to any other suit and so East
plays the ♠2, low-encouraging, to ask for a spade continuation.

Notice how encourage-discourage signals help West find the
winning defence. If East-West play count signals only, there is no
way West can tell which defence to adopt.

In our view, encourage-discourage signals are the most important
ones in defence. In the previous 15-20 years many top players
switched to count as their primary signalling method. Nowadays
players are returning to the good old methods of like-it, hate-it. Of
course, these need to be modified in specific situations, especially
for defence in the middle part of a deal.

Dealer North : Both vulnerable	Here is a deal, from long ago, which featured Krzysztof Wagrodzki, a leading Polish player at the time.

NORTH
♠ K 7
♡ 9 6 4
◇ A Q
♣ K Q 10 9 3 2

WEST
♠ Q J 6 5 3
♡ K 3
◇ 9 8 2
♣ 7 6 5

West	North	East	South
Pass	1♣	Pass	1♡
Pass	2♣	Pass	3♡
Pass	4♡	All pass	

West led the ♠Q and South, Wagrodzki, played low from dummy. East followed with the ♠2, low-like. What should West do at trick 2?

NORTH
♠ K 7
♡ 9 6 4
◇ A Q
♣ K Q 10 9 3 2

WEST
♠ Q J 6 5 3
♡ K 3
◇ 9 8 2
♣ 7 6 5

EAST
♠ A 9 8 2
♡ 7 5
◇ J 10 7 6 3
♣ A 4

SOUTH
♠ 10 4
♡ A Q J 10 8 2
◇ K 5 4
♣ J 8

The full deal is on the left.

After lengthy thought West shifted to a low diamond, hoping to find East with the ◇K. South took the ◇A, cashed the ◇Q, crossed to the ♡A and played the ◇K, pitching the ♠K from dummy. 4♡ made.

Why did West shift to a diamond? West wondered why South had ducked the spade at trick 1 and thought that South might have the hand below:

♠ 10 4   ♡ A Q J 10 8 2   ◇ J 5 4   ♣ A 8

If so, a diamond switch at trick 2 was essential. Another spade would put East on lead and declarer would be able to draw trumps and use the clubs to discard the diamond losers.

How can West solve this dilemma? By trusting partner. On the actual deal East's ♠2 asked West to continue spades and so West should obey. If South held the other hand, East would have the ◇K and would discourage spades. Then a diamond switch would be right. Honour thy partner and do not mastermind the situation.

Remember, a discouraging signal does not merely say you have nothing of value in the suit led. It conveys much more. It tells partner to discontinue that suit and find the necessary switch for the deadly defence.

Using encourage-discourage signals, you will have no problem knowing what to do at trick 2 on each of the next two deals:

	NORTH				NORTH		
	♠ Q 5				♠ Q 5		
	♡ Q J 8				♡ Q J 8		
	◇ A 8 6 3				◇ A 8 6 3		
	♣ 9 6 5 2				♣ 9 6 5 2		
WEST		EAST		WEST		EAST	
♠ A K J 10 7 4		♠ 9 2		♠ A K J 10 7 4		♠ 9 2	
♡ 7 5		♡ A 4 3		♡ 7 5		♡ K 4	
◇ 9 4 2		◇ Q J 10 5		◇ 9 4 2		◇ K 10 7 5	
♣ 8 4		♣ Q 10 7 3		♣ 8 4		♣ Q J 10 7 3	
	SOUTH				SOUTH		
	♠ 8 6 3				♠ 8 6 3		
	♡ K 10 9 6 2				♡ A 10 9 6 3 2		
	◇ K 7				◇ Q J		
	♣ A K J				♣ A K		

West	North	East	South
			1♡
2♠	3♡	Pass	4♡
Pass	Pass	Pass	

West leads the ♠A in each case. What next?

Imagine two beginners are East-West. After playing the ♠A West will wonder, 'What now? Do I continue spades or switch to a trump?' That is the crux of the problem.

To defeat 4♡, it is vital in (A) to switch to trumps; in (B) West needs to continue spades. In (A) East discourages a spade continuation by playing the ♠9 and West switches to a trump. That is easy, isn't it?

East ducks the first heart. If South plays another spade West wins and continues with a heart. Now East takes the ♡A and plays a third round. South cannot avoid one down.

If West plays a second spade in (A), South can ruff the spade loser and make the contract via the club finesse.

In (B) East encourages a spade continuation (♠2). West obeys and plays ♠K and a third spade. East over-ruffs dummy and exits with a heart or a club. Eventually East scores the ◇K for one down.

Notice that if East-West are playing count signals, East in each case will play ♠2, lowest to show a doubleton. That gives West no help whatsoever in finding the winning defence. If East instead plays the ♠9 (high-low to show an odd number), West will cash another spade. Now declarer will succeed each time. In (A) South can ruff the spade loser and in (B) West will not continue spades to allow East to over-ruff dummy.

What if East plays the ♠9 and it is a singleton? Now it is urgent for West to shift to a trump. If East's ♠9 is bare, South began with four spades and West needs to reduce dummy's ruffing power. A trump at trick 2 and another when in with the next spade leaves dummy with only one trump to ruff South's spade losers.
It is important not to be too smug. Sometimes count signals can be useful and even more helpful than encouraging-discouraging signals. You will find details about that in the next chapter and also in Chapter 13: *Interpretation of partner's signals*.

Chapter 3
Count signals

When partner leads a suit, we advise reverse attitude signals (low-encourage, high-discourage). When declarer leads a suit, use reverse count (lowest = even number, high-low = odd number).

NORTH	West	North	East	South

NORTH
♠ J 6
♡ 10 4 3
◇ J 10 9 7
♣ A Q J 4

EAST
♠ K 2
♡ 9 7 5
◇ A 6 5 4 3 2
♣ 10 7

West	North	East	South
			1♠
Pass	1NT	Pass	2♠
Pass	3♠	Pass	4♠
Pass	Pass	Pass	

Partner leads the ♡2 against 4♠. South wins with the ♡J and plays the ♣6 next. West follows with the ♣2, ♣Q from dummy. What do you do when declarer calls for the ◇J from dummy?

Answer: From West's lead of the ♡2, fourth-highest, you know the layout of the hearts. South has three. West's count signal on the clubs was the ♣2, lowest to show an even number of clubs. As South should have six spades for the 2♠ rebid, you can place South with a 6-3-1-3 pattern. Therefore you must play the ◇A. The South hand:

♠ Q 9 7 5 4 3 ♡ A K J ◇ K ♣ K 6 5

To determine declarer's exact shape, we take into account not only the count card in clubs, but also the inference from the opening lead. It is helpful when partner's opening lead indicates the number of cards held in that suit.

The next example shows how a defender, after winning a trick in the suit led by partner, can let partner know the number of cards remaining when returning the suit.

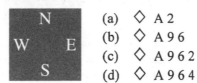

♦ Q J 10

(a) ♦ A 2
(b) ♦ A 9 6
(c) ♦ A 9 6 2
(d) ♦ A 9 6 4 2

West leads the ♦Q. East wins with the ♦A and returns lowest to show an even number originally, the ♦2 in (a) and (c), or the highest to show an odd number originally, the ♦9 in (b) and (d).

The same applies when a defender is following suit:

<table>
<tr><td colspan="2">

NORTH
♠ A 5
♡ 10 7 3
♦ K Q J 9
♣ A 7 5 2

WEST
♠ Q 8
♡ K J 9 2
♦ 8 7 3 2
♣ 10 6 4

</td><td>

West	North	East	South
	1♦	Pass	1♠
Pass	1NT	Pass	4♠
Pass	Pass	Pass	

You chose an attacking lead with the ♡2. Partner played the ♡Q, taken by the ♡A. South led the ♠3 to the ace, followed by the ♠5 to the jack and your queen. Partner followed with the ♠6-then-♠2. What now?

</td></tr>
</table>

To have any hope of defeating 4♠, partner must have the ♦A. Two possible hand-types for declarer matter:

(a)   ♠ K J 9 7 4 3   ♡ A 8 6   ♦ 4   ♣ K Q 8
(b)   ♠ K J 9 7 4 3   ♡ A 6   ♦ 6 5 4   ♣ Q J

If South has (a), you should cash two hearts and the ♦A. If (b), you must cash only one heart and then shift to a club. How can you tell?

Play the ♡K and note the card partner plays. There is no problem if partner gives you accurate count. It will then be clear what to do.

From an original holding of ♡Q-8-5-4, partner should play the ♡4 (showing an even number of hearts), while from ♡Q-5-4, partner plays the ♡5, top from the remaining doubleton and showing an odd number originally. Do not worry about South having started with four hearts. If so, South would have explored the possibility of a 4-4 heart fit.

This situation has a similar theme:

South dealer : Both vulnerable

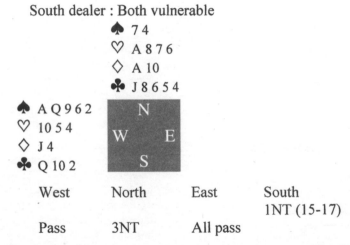

♠ 7 4
♡ A 8 7 6
♢ A 10
♣ J 8 6 5 4

♠ A Q 9 6 2
♡ 10 5 4
♢ J 4
♣ Q 10 2

West	North	East	South
			1NT (15-17)
Pass	3NT	All pass	

You lead the ♠6: four – ten – jack. South continued with the ♣A, ♣K and ♣3. East followed twice and then discarded the ♠3. What do you do at trick 5?

Answer: Partner's ♠3 discard is the lowest spade and tells you that partner began with an even number of spades. In this case it will be four. If partner started with two spades, partner would not discard the only spade left. Do not try to find partner's entry. Play the ♠A and collect four more tricks, since declarer's hand is:

♠ K J   ♡ K 3 2   ♢ K 9 8 3 2   ♣ A K 3

When the contract is at the five-level or higher, count signals should take priority over encourage-discourage signals.

North dealer : Nil vulnerable

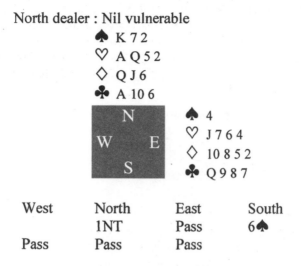

♠ K 7 2
♡ A Q 5 2
♢ Q J 6
♣ A 10 6

♠ 4
♡ J 7 6 4
♢ 10 8 5 2
♣ Q 9 8 7

West	North	East	South
	1NT	Pass	6♠
Pass	Pass	Pass	

West leads the ♢K. What do you play as East?

Answer: Did you notice that partner has led the king from A-K? The normal card is the ace, top of touching honours. The king is the correct card here, because in many cases one would lead the ace against a slam even without holding the king.

Although the king is also led from a K-Q-high suit, this would not give partner much of a problem in a slam contract. We have come to the conclusion that when the contract is at the five-level or higher, we lead second-top from touching honours: the king from an A-K suit, the queen from a K-Q suit, and so on.

Therefore, in this problem, East should play the ♢2, giving count (reverse count, as we recommend it).

Chapter 4
Ducking in defence

Everyone knows how a declarer can score extra tricks and make a contract by ducking a trick. Ducking plays are also available to the defenders. A well-conceived duck might disrupt declarer's communications, cut declarer off from a number of tricks or mislead declarer as to the location of critical cards. It might also help your side by providing extra communication with partner.

Here are some examples how a well-timed duck can neutralize the value of a long suit in dummy:

South dealer : Nil vulnerable

```
                NORTH
                ♠ 5 3
                ♡ K 7 4
                ◇ K J 10 8 7
                ♣ 9 7 3
WEST                        EAST
♠ J 10 9 8 2                ♠ 7 6 4
♡ J 8                       ♡ Q 10 9 6
◇ 5 4 2                     ◇ A Q 6
♣ K Q 5                     ♣ 10 8 6
                SOUTH
                ♠ A K Q
                ♡ A 5 3 2
                ◇ 9 3
                ♣ A J 4 2
```

After 1NT : 3NT, West leads the ♠J. South wins, leads the ◇9 and plays low in dummy. East must let the ◇9 win. If East takes the first diamond, South can set up the rest of the diamonds, with the ♡K entry, and make ten tricks. See what happens if East ducks the ◇9. South plays another diamond to the ◇8 and East wins with the ◇Q. South lacks the entries to establish the diamonds. A heart to the king allows South to set up two diamond winners in dummy, but there is no access to them. Dummy's diamonds are dead and declarer cannot make more than eight tricks.

South dealer : Nil vulnerable

NORTH
- ♠ A 6 4
- ♡ 8 2
- ◊ K Q 10 9 6 3
- ♣ 8 3

WEST
- ♠ J 9 3
- ♡ Q 9 4 3
- ◊ A 5 4
- ♣ K J 2

EAST
- ♠ 10 8 5 2
- ♡ J 7 5
- ◊ J 8
- ♣ Q 7 6 5

SOUTH
- ♠ K Q 7
- ♡ A K 10 6
- ◊ 7 2
- ♣ A 10 9 4

After 1NT : 3NT, West leads the ♡3. South captures East's ♡J with the ♡K and plays the ◊2. West plays low and, to establish the diamonds, declarer inserts the ◊10 from dummy. East has to duck smoothly. South will now return to hand with a spade and lead the next diamond. Of course, West must play low again.

Having placed the ◊J with West, perhaps ◊A-J-x-x, South will now finesse the ◊9. East wins with the ◊J and dummy's diamonds are waste paper.

In no-trumps, when declarer has a doubleton opposite a long suit in dummy which has only one entry outside the long suit, there are many positions where a duck is essential.

$$◊ \ K \ J \ 8 \ 7 \ 3$$
$$◊ \ Q \ 6 \ 2 \qquad\qquad ◊ \ A \ 10 \ 4$$
$$◊ \ 9 \ 5$$

In this situation, if South leads the nine, low, low, East should duck even though this could cost a trick. South is highly likely to continue with the ◊5 to dummy's eight. Now you collect your ◊10 and dummy's suit is finished unless declarer has two outside entries to dummy. If you take the ◊10 on the first round, declarer can set up the rest of the suit and needs only one entry to dummy.

If West plays the ◊Q on South's ◊9, East should definitely duck if declarer plays the ◊K from dummy.

♣ K 10 9 8 4 2

♣ A 7 5   ♣ J 6

♣ Q 3

If dummy has only one outside entry and South leads the ♣3 to dummy's ♣10, East should duck. If East takes the ♣10, South can overtake the ♣Q with the ♣K next time and force out the ♣A. If East ducks the ♣10, South has to guess how to continue the clubs.

A low club will work if either defender started with ♣A-x. If East had ducked the ♣10 and declarer plays low from dummy, playing East or West for ♣A-x, West ducks the ♣Q and dummy's clubs are worthless. If declarer plays the ♣K from dummy and runs into ♣A-x, again dummy's clubs are useless. However, if East takes the ♣10 on the first round South has no problems.

♣ K J 10 8 5 3

♣ A 7 2   ♣ Q 6

♣ 9 4

By now we all know that if declarer leads the ♣9 and lets it run, East must duck. South will almost certainly continue with a club to the ten or jack and dummy's long suit is neutralised.

To duck is easier in theory than at the table. See what happened on this deal from the semi-finals of the USA Playoffs:

North dealer : Nil vulnerable

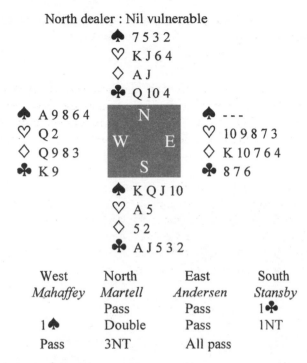

♠ 7 5 3 2
♡ K J 6 4
◇ A J
♣ Q 10 4

♠ A 9 8 6 4
♡ Q 2
◇ Q 9 8 3
♣ K 9

♠ - - -
♡ 10 9 8 7 3
◇ K 10 7 6 4
♣ 8 7 6

♠ K Q J 10
♡ A 5
◇ 5 2
♣ A J 5 3 2

West	North	East	South
Mahaffey	*Martell*	*Andersen*	*Stansby*
	Pass	Pass	1♣
1♠	Double	Pass	1NT
Pass	3NT	All pass	

West led the ♠6. South won, crossed to the ♡K and led the
♣Q: six – two – king. West switched to a low diamond, taken by
the ◇A in dummy. To cash the clubs would leave South with only
eight tricks. Hoping for a miracle in hearts, Lew Stansby played a
heart to his ace next. When the ♡Q dropped, dummy's ♡J was
high. South crossed to the ♣10, cashed the ♡J and had nine tricks.

Suppose West ducks the ♣Q. Won't South repeat the club finesse?
If he runs the ♣10 next, West wins and shifts to a diamond. Now
there is no entry to dummy's ♡J even if South plays off the ♡A.

What if South plays the ♣4 to the ♣J after the ♣Q scores? West
wins and shifts to a diamond. Declarer can win, but cannot come
to nine tricks.

When the ♡A drops the ♡Q, South can cross to the ♣10 to reach the ♡J, but then has no entry back to hand for the clubs. Declarer cannot enjoy both the clubs and the ♡J.

Even the greatest of champions can err. On the next example Terence Reese slipped from grace:

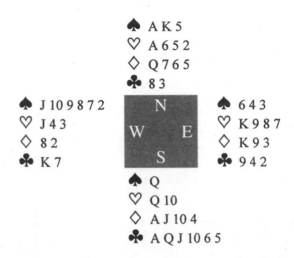

♠ A K 5
♡ A 6 5 2
♢ Q 7 6 5
♣ 8 3

♠ J 10 9 8 7 2
♡ J 4 3
♢ 8 2
♣ K 7

♠ 6 4 3
♡ K 9 8 7
♢ K 9 3
♣ 9 4 2

♠ Q
♡ Q 10
♢ A J 10 4
♣ A Q J 10 6 5

Paul Chemla of France was South in 6♣ on the ♠J lead. Chemla took the ♠A in dummy and finessed the ♣Q. Terence Reese won with the ♣K and switched to a heart. End of story. Declarer took the ♡A, discarded the heart loser on the ♠K and could take the diamond finesse. When that succeeded, the slam was home.

Suppose West had ducked the ♣Q. South could still succeed, but the odds are that he would rely on the ♣K being with East. After a heart to the ace, ♠K ditching a heart, South would repeat the club finesse. West wins and South is saddled with a diamond loser later for one down.

On the next deal from a match between England and the USA, Charles Goren produced a classic coup with a duck in declarer's side suit:

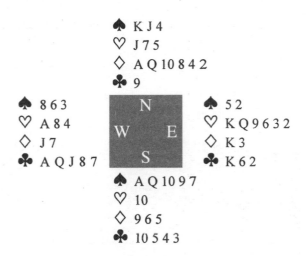

```
              ♠ K J 4
              ♡ J 7 5
              ◇ A Q 10 8 4 2
              ♣ 9
♠ 8 6 3          N          ♠ 5 2
♡ A 8 4       W     E       ♡ K Q 9 6 3 2
◇ J 7                       ◇ K 3
♣ A Q J 8 7      S          ♣ K 6 2
              ♠ A Q 10 9 7
              ♡ 10
              ◇ 9 6 5
              ♣ 10 5 4 3
```

South was in 4♠ doubled. West led the ♡A and a second heart. South ruffed and played a diamond to dummy's ◇10. Goren, East, ducked. Figuring that West must have started with ◇K-J-7, South drew trumps and played a diamond to the queen. East won with the ◇K and promptly cashed four club tricks.

South should have done better. Cash only two rounds of trumps before finessing the ◇Q. Even if this is ruffed, South can lose only one heart, one diamond and one club. However, South was so confident of the diamond position he wanted to score the overtrick.

The next deal has a slightly different theme:

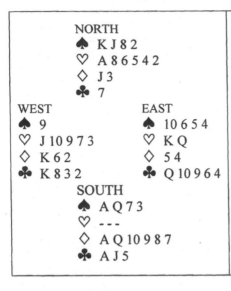

South plays 6♠ on the ♡10 lead (underleading). South discarded a club on the ♡A and led the ◇J, finessing. If West takes the ◇K, South makes 6♠ easily. He can ruff the club loser, draw trumps and South's hand is high.

If West ducks the ◇J smoothly and South repeats the diamond finesse, West wins and plays a third diamond. South has to ruff high in dummy. Declarer can still succeed double dummy, but why should South pick East to have four trumps?

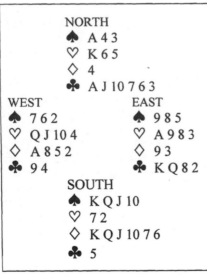

On this deal, Boris Shapiro of England shone in defence.

South was in 4♠ and West began with the ♡Q, followed by the ♡J and a third heart, king, ace, ruffed. To set up his side suit, South led the ◇K and Shapiro, West, ducked. He also ducked the ◇Q next and also the ◇J. East ruffed the third diamond and played a fourth heart, giving South a totally useless ruff-and-discard. There was no way for declarer to make the contract, no matter in which hand the heart ruff was taken.

NORTH
♠ 9 4
♡ 9 7 3
◇ J 7 4 3
♣ A K 8 2

WEST
♠ K 10 6 5
♡ 4
◇ 10 9 8
♣ J 10 7 4 3

EAST
♠ 8 3 2
♡ 10 8 5 2
◇ Q 6 5 2
♣ Q 5

SOUTH
♠ A Q J 7
♡ A K Q J 6
◇ A K
♣ 9 6

South is playing 6♡ on the ◇10 lead. South won, cashed the ♡A, crossed to the ♣A and led a spade to the queen. West ducked. South returned to dummy with a club to the king and then finessed the ♠J. West won and played the ♣J, on which East discarded the third spade.

Declarer was doomed. If he tried to ruff a spade, East would over-ruff and if he drew trumps he would be left with a spade loser.

NORTH
♠ A J 7 4 3
♡ J
◇ A K J 6
♣ 10 7 6

WEST
♠ 5 2
♡ A 10 7 5
◇ 10 9
♣ Q 9 8 5 3

EAST
♠ K Q 10 8 6
♡ 6 3 2
◇ 8 4 2
♣ 4 2

SOUTH
♠ 9
♡ K Q 9 8 4
◇ Q 7 5 3
♣ A K J

Here is a really great defence by Gabriel Chagas, one of the world's best players.

South was in 6◇ and West, Chagas, led the ♠5.

South took dummy's ♠A and led the ♡J: two, four . . . Chagas ducked! South could no longer make the slam.

If West takes the ♡A and plays a diamond, best, South wins with the ◇A, ruffs a spade low, ruffs a low heart, ruffs a spade with the ◇Q and draw trumps. He scores one spade, three hearts, four diamonds in dummy, two ruffs in hand and two top clubs.

This deal arose in the 1981 European Championships:

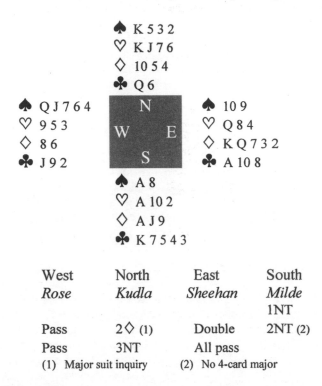

♠ K 5 3 2
♡ K J 7 6
◇ 10 5 4
♣ Q 6

♠ Q J 7 6 4   ♠ 10 9
♡ 9 5 3   ♡ Q 8 4
◇ 8 6   ◇ K Q 7 3 2
♣ J 9 2   ♣ A 10 8

♠ A 8
♡ A 10 2
◇ A J 9
♣ K 7 5 4 3

West	North	East	South
Rose	*Kudla*	*Sheehan*	*Milde*
			1NT
Pass	2◇ (1)	Double	2NT (2)
Pass	3NT	All pass	
(1) Major suit inquiry		(2) No 4-card major	

West led the ◇8. East played low and South won with the ◇J. Declarer played a club to the ♣Q and Sheehan ducked. On the ♣6, East played the ♣10. South played low and so did West. East continued with the ◇K, ducked, followed by another diamond, taken by South.

Milde could still make 3NT double dummy (cross to the ♠A and finesse the ♡10). However, he placed the ♣A with West and thought a third club was safe. He was soon disappointed. East took the third club and cashed two more diamonds for one down.

This deal also occurred in the 1981 European Open Teams Championship. This time the hero was Tony Forrester, a team-mate of Rose and Sheehan:

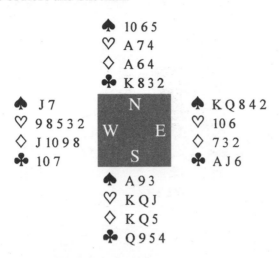

♠ 10 6 5
♡ A 7 4
◇ A 6 4
♣ K 8 3 2

♠ J 7   ♠ K Q 8 4 2
♡ 9 8 5 3 2   ♡ 10 6
◇ J 10 9 8   ◇ 7 3 2
♣ 10 7   ♣ A J 6

♠ A 9 3
♡ K Q J
◇ K Q 5
♣ Q 9 5 4

After 1NT South, 3NT North, West led the ◇J. South won with the ◇K and played a club to the king. Forrester, East, could see from his own values and those in dummy, that West would have very little. The best hope was to find West with the ♣J, but what if the ♣J was doubleton? If East captured the ♣K and switched to a spade, South could duck till the third round and then play the clubs to avoid East coming on lead.

Having seen all this in the blink of an eye, Forrester let dummy's ♣K hold. South continued with a club and Forrester played the ♣J. Believing West had the ♣A and East had played the ♣J from J-10-x perhaps, South ducked the ♣J.

Now Forrester shifted to a low spade, ducked to the jack. The spade return was ducked and the third spade dislodged South's ♠A. When the third club was played, a surprised South found East winning the trick and cashing two more spades for one down.

Finding the right moment to duck may lead declarer into a losing line. Witness this deal:

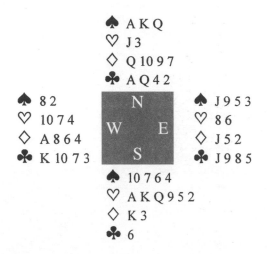

♠ A K Q
♡ J 3
◇ Q 10 9 7
♣ A Q 4 2

♠ 8 2
♡ 10 7 4
◇ A 8 6 4
♣ K 10 7 3

♠ J 9 5 3
♡ 8 6
◇ J 5 2
♣ J 9 8 5

♠ 10 7 6 4
♡ A K Q 9 5 2
◇ K 3
♣ 6

South played in 6♡. West led the ♣3. South rose with the ♣A, cashed three rounds of trumps, followed by a spade to dummy and the ◇7 to the ◇K. West ducked. When South continued with the ◇3, West ducked again and South naturally finessed the ◇10. East won and the slam could no longer be made.

If West had taken the ◇K with the ace, South could succeed via a diamond to the queen and a third diamond. East's ◇J is ruffed and dummy's diamond winner takes care of South's spade loser. Double dummy South could always make the slam, but West's duck lured South into a line that failed.

Here is Italy's Benito Garozzo in action in the final of a World Championship:

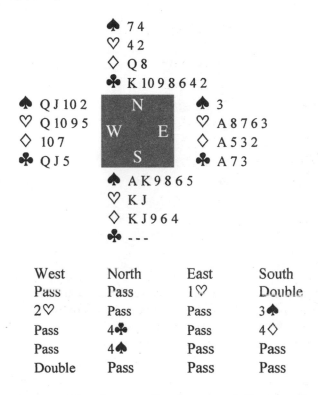

```
              ♠ 7 4
              ♡ 4 2
              ◇ Q 8
              ♣ K 10 9 8 6 4 2
  ♠ Q J 10 2          N           ♠ 3
  ♡ Q 10 9 5    W          E      ♡ A 8 7 6 3
  ◇ 10 7                           ◇ A 5 3 2
  ♣ Q J 5              S           ♣ A 7 3
              ♠ A K 9 8 6 5
              ♡ K J
              ◇ K J 9 6 4
              ♣ - - -
```

West	North	East	South
Pass	Pass	1♡	Double
2♡	Pass	Pass	3♠
Pass	4♣	Pass	4◇
Pass	4♠	Pass	Pass
Double	Pass	Pass	Pass

West began with a heart to East's ace and Garozzo returned a trump. South won with the ♣A and played a low diamond to the queen. Garozzo ducked! When the ◇8 came from dummy, Garozzo ducked again!

Placing the ◇A with West, South inserted the ◇9 and a surprised West won with the ◇10. West continued with a trump and South finished two down. If Garozzo had taken the ◇Q with the ace, declarer can keep it to one down.

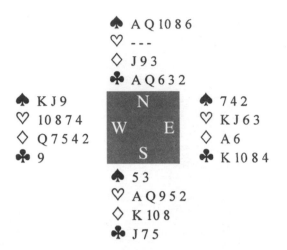

♠ A Q 10 8 6
♡ - - -
◇ J 9 3
♣ A Q 6 3 2

♠ K J 9
♡ 10 8 7 4
◇ Q 7 5 4 2
♣ 9

♠ 7 4 2
♡ K J 6 3
◇ A 6
♣ K 10 8 4

♠ 5 3
♡ A Q 9 5 2
◇ K 10 8
♣ J 7 5

This deal arose in the Sunday Times Tournament, 1991. At every
table South was in 3NT and every West began with a low
diamond. East took the ◇A and returned a diamond. South
ducked this to West's ◇Q and won the diamond return.

South continued with the ♣5 to dummy's queen. Every East but
one took the ♣K and returned the ♣10. South won with the ♣J
and led the ♠3: nine – ten – two. When this succeeded, declarer
played the ♣A and exited with a club to East. With only major
suit cards left, East was finished. A spade return was futile and a
heart gave South the entry to play the spade again. South thus lost
just two diamonds and two clubs.

Only one defender, the brilliant Gabriel Chagas of Brazil, ducked
when declarer played a club to the queen. South now hoped West
had ♣K doubleton and cashed the ♣A. He exited with a third
club. Chagas won with the ♣K, cashed the ♣10 and led a spade.

Dummy won and South could cash a club, but after the ♠A and
another spade, West was in. He took two diamond tricks and
South was three down.

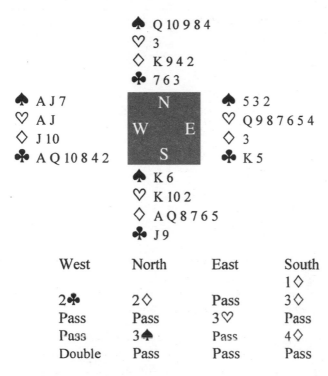

♠ Q 10 9 8 4
♡ 3
◇ K 9 4 2
♣ 7 6 3

♠ A J 7
♡ A J
◇ J 10
♣ A Q 10 8 4 2

♠ 5 3 2
♡ Q 9 8 7 6 5 4
◇ 3
♣ K 5

♠ K 6
♡ K 10 2
◇ A Q 8 7 6 5
♣ J 9

West	North	East	South
			1◇
2♣	2◇	Pass	3◇
Pass	Pass	3♡	Pass
Pass	3♠	Pass	4◇
Double	Pass	Pass	Pass

Sometimes it is vital to duck because we cannot tell which suit to play next. West led the ◇J, taken by the ◇K. Next came the ♠4: five from East, king from South. To beat 4◇ West needs to find East with the ♡K or the ♣K, but which one? If East has the ♡K, West must lead the ♡J to East's king for a club lead through South. If East has the ♣K, West can simply cash two clubs and the ♡A. If West takes the ♠A at once, it is a pure guess what to do next. So far, from East's ♠5, West can place East with either ♠6-5 doubleton or ♠5-3-2 (playing reverse count). When South plays the next spade, West takes the ♠A and watches East's spade closely. With the ♠3-2 left, East should play the ♠3 if holding the ♡K (higher card for the higher suit) and the ♠2 if holding the ♣K (bottom card for the lowest suit).

NORTH
♠ 8 6 4
♡ 2
♢ A K 10 4
♣ Q J 9 8 2

WEST
♠ J 10 9 7 3 2
♡ 8 6
♢ J 2
♣ A 10 4

EAST
♠ K Q
♡ Q J 9 7 4 3
♢ Q 9 6
♣ 7 3

SOUTH
♠ A 5
♡ A K 10 5
♢ 8 7 5 3
♣ K 6 5

On this deal West again needs to duck with an ace, but for a different reason:
South is in 3NT. West leads the ♠J and South captures East's ♠Q. South plays the ♣K, ducked, followed by another club, also ducked. On the third club, East pitched the blocking ♠K. West won and cashed five more spades for two down.

For this defence Leinoe (East) – Nieminen (West) won the Brilliancy Prize at the European Championships.

NORTH
♠ Q 6 5
♡ 10 9 4
♢ A K 10 9
♣ J 10 9

WEST
♠ J 10 9 2
♡ Q J 6
♢ 5 3 2
♣ 4 3 2

EAST
♠ 7 4
♡ 7 5 3 2
♢ 7 6 4
♣ A 8 7 6

SOUTH
♠ A K 8 3
♡ A K 8
♢ Q J 8
♣ K Q 5

On this deal, East ducked in order to prevent declarer from implementing a squeeze:
South was in 6NT on the ♠J lead. He won with the ♠A and played the ♣K. East ducked. If East takes the ♣A early, South will play off the minor suit winners and on the last minor winner, West is squeezed in spades and hearts.
South continued with the ♣Q and East ducked again. The result? The squeeze has now evaporated. If South plays a third club, East takes two club tricks, of course. If South cashes the diamonds, West can throw the idle third club.

On this deal a duck was needed to give declarer a losing option:

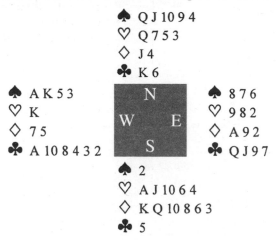

♠ Q J 10 9 4
♥ Q 7 5 3
♦ J 4
♣ K 6

♠ A K 5 3　　　　　　　♠ 8 7 6
♥ K　　　　　　　　　　♥ 9 8 2
♦ 7 5　　　　　　　　　♦ A 9 2
♣ A 10 8 4 3 2　　　　　♣ Q J 9 7

♠ 2
♥ A J 10 6 4
♦ K Q 10 8 6 3
♣ 5

This deal arose in a tournament in Monte Carlo. The auction at almost every table went like this:

West	North	East	South
			1◇
2♣	2♠	3♣	3♡
4♣	4♡	All pass	

In each case West began with the ♠A, ♣A, followed by the ♠K. South ruffed and played a diamond to the jack. Every East bar one took the ◇A. With no entry to dummy, declarer had no choice but to lay down the ♡A. When the ♡K appeared, 4♡ made.

Eddie Kantar was the sole defender who ducked the ◇J. He asked himself why declarer wanted to get to dummy. If it was to take a finesse in trumps, Kantar saw no reason to deprive South of the opportunity. Happy to have reached dummy, declarer led the ♡Q: two – four – king and the contract was one down, as East still had to score the ◇A.

The same theme occurred on this deal, from the 2007 World Championships, but in a more dramatic context:

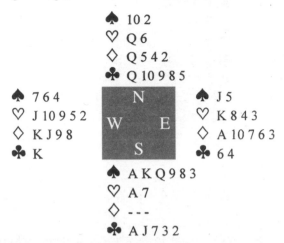

```
                  ♠ 10 2
                  ♡ Q 6
                  ◇ Q 5 4 2
                  ♣ Q 10 9 8 5
    ♠ 7 6 4          N          ♠ J 5
    ♡ J 10 9 5 2              ♡ K 8 4 3
    ◇ K J 9 8   W       E     ◇ A 10 7 6 3
    ♣ K           S          ♣ 6 4
                  ♠ A K Q 9 8 3
                  ♡ A 7
                  ◇ - - -
                  ♣ A J 7 3 2
```

In the quarter-finals, five tables reached 7♣ by South and received the ♡J lead. In the Seniors Bowl the play was identical at every table: ♡J – queen – king – ace, followed by the ♣A. Making 7♣. The same took place in the Bermuda Bowl when Norway bid 7♣.

In the Venice Cup, Michelle Brunner, England, was East when China played 7♣ on the ♡J lead. Declarer played dummy's ♡Q and it held the trick! Grateful to be in dummy, declarer took the club finesse.

That was one down and 13 Imps to England instead of 17 to China, when England played in 4♠ at the other table. South might have wondered why West would lead the ♡J from a K-J-10 suit against a grand slam, but this is no way deflects from Brunner's brilliant duck, which deservedly earned her the International Bridge Press Association Defence of the Year Award.

To finish this chapter, here is a classic deal from the Switzerland vs Netherlands match in a European Open Teams Championship:

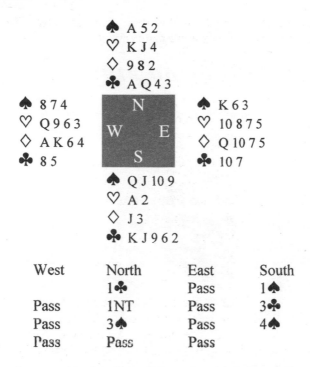

West	North	East	South
	1♣	Pass	1♠
Pass	1NT	Pass	3♣
Pass	3♠	Pass	4♠
Pass	Pass	Pass	

West began with the ◇A, ◇K and a third diamond, ruffed by South. Declarer ran the ♠Q and East, Jean Besse, ducked. Next came the ♠J, low, low, and Besse ducked again!

To cater for West holding ♠K-x-x-x, South started on the clubs. He could afford West to ruff the third round as he could then draw West's last trump. If West led another diamond after ruffing the third club, South could ruff in hand, cross to the ♡K and play the ♠A to capture West's ♠K.

All followed to two rounds of clubs and, sure enough, West ruffed the third club. On this Besse threw his last diamond. When West continued with the fourth diamond, heart discard from dummy, a highly disappointed South saw East ruff with the ♠K. One down.

Chapter 5
Surround plays

The best way to illustrate this technique is by an example:

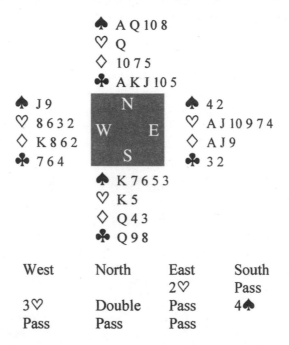

	♠ A Q 10 8		
	♡ Q		
	◇ 10 7 5		
	♣ A K J 10 5		

♠ J 9   ♠ 4 2
♡ 8 6 3 2   ♡ A J 10 9 7 4
◇ K 8 6 2   ◇ A J 9
♣ 7 6 4   ♣ 3 2

♠ K 7 6 5 3
♡ K 5
◇ Q 4 3
♣ Q 9 8

West	North	East	South
		2♡	Pass
3♡	Double	Pass	4♠
Pass	Pass	Pass	

Against 4♠ West leads a heart and East wins with the ace. How should East continue?

There are no tricks for the defence in spades or clubs and East can tell the only chance is in diamonds. East must shift to a diamond at once. If not, South draws trumps and pitches two diamonds on dummy's clubs. East must hope that West has the ◇K. If so, which diamond should East lead?

If East plays the ♢A followed by a low one, South can play low on the second round and lose only two tricks. If East starts with the ♢9, again South can play low and lose only two diamonds. The only card to give the defence three diamond tricks is the ♢J. If South plays low, the ♢J wins and East continues with the ♢9. West takes the ♢K and returns a diamond to East's ♢A. If South covers the ♢J, West captures the ♢Q and returns a diamond. East now has the ♢A-9 over dummy's ten and takes two tricks.

If South has the ♢K there is no genuine defence to beat 4♠. Still, the switch to the ♢J might work if South began with ♢K-x-x. Perhaps South thinks you have made a deceptive lead from ♢Q-J-x and ducks the ♢J. When you play the ♢9 next, maybe South ducks once more. Suddenly you have three diamond tricks and South is one down. Naturally East plays the same way, ♢J first, if holding ♢K-J-9.

How can you recognise this situation? The standard position is that you are sitting over dummy and you have a high card in dummy surrounded, plus a non-touching higher honour as well. In that case, lead the card just above dummy's high card that you have surrounded. For example:

```
              North
              A 9 3
West                      East
K 5 4                     Q 10 8 2
              South
              J 7 6
```

If East wishes to attack this suit, East should start with the ten. East has dummy's nine surrounded, and the queen is the non-touching higher honour. If East leads the ten, South can make only one trick. If East starts with any other card, the defence cannot score two tricks. If East leads the two or the eight, South can make two tricks. The same would apply (lead the ten first) if East had K-10-8 and West has Q-x-x-x.

The surround play occurred on this deal from a tournament in Deauville, France. The defenders were Martin Hoffman and the famous English player, Rixi Markus:

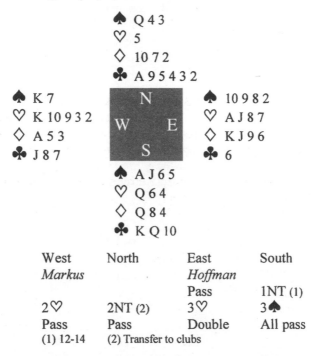

<pre>
              ♠ Q 4 3
              ♡ 5
              ◇ 10 7 2
              ♣ A 9 5 4 3 2
♠ K 7   ♠ 10 9 8 2
♡ K 10 9 3 2   N   ♡ A J 8 7
◇ A 5 3   W   E   ◇ K J 9 6
♣ J 8 7   ♣ 6
                    S
              ♠ A J 6 5
              ♡ Q 6 4
              ◇ Q 8 4
              ♣ K Q 10
</pre>

West	North	East	South
Markus		*Hoffman*	
		Pass	1NT (1)
2♡	2NT (2)	3♡	3♠
Pass	Pass	Double	All pass

(1) 12-14   (2) Transfer to clubs

West led the ♡3. Hoffman took the ♡A and instantly switched to the ◇J: queen – ace. West returned a diamond: ten – king. East cashed the ◇9 and returned a heart, ruffed in dummy. A club to the king was followed by South's last heart, ruffed in dummy.

Declarer played the ♠Q, ducked to West's ♠K. West returned a club, ruffed by East. When East played the ◇6, the thirteenth diamond, this promoted an extra trump trick for the defence. If South ruffed low, West would over-ruff. If South ruffed high, East had another trump trick. East's switch to the ◇J at trick 2 is an excellent example of the surround play in practice.

Here is another layout where a surround lead is needed.

```
              North
              9 4 3
West                      East
K 7 5                     Q 10 8 6
              South
              A J 2
```

If East switches to a low card, South can duck in hand and make two tricks. If East leads the ten, declarer is held to one trick and the defenders score all the tricks to which they are entitled. The ten is still the right card if East has K-10-8-x and West has Q-x-x.

Sometimes you do not have an exact surround position, but it is still correct to lead the 'surround' card:

```
              North
              10 4 3
                          East
                          K J 8 2
```

If East is on lead and intends to switch to this suit, the right card is the jack, even though the J-8 does not exactly surround dummy's ten. Perhaps the full layout is like this:

```
              North
              10 4 3
West                      East
A 9 5                     K J 8 2
              South
              Q 7 6
```

As partner holds the nine, leading the jack enables the defence to take all their tricks.

However, leading the jack does not come with guarantees. Mostly it is the correct card, but there are exceptions. Consider this:

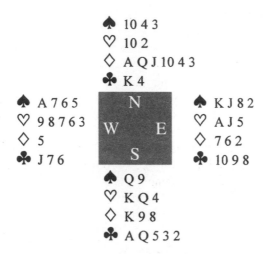

```
              ♠ 10 4 3
              ♡ 10 2
              ◇ A Q J 10 4 3
              ♣ K 4
   ♠ A 7 6 5      N        ♠ K J 8 2
   ♡ 9 8 7 6 3  W   E      ♡ A J 5
   ◇ 5                     ◇ 7 6 2
   ♣ J 7 6         S       ♣ 10 9 8
              ♠ Q 9
              ♡ K Q 4
              ◇ K 9 8
              ♣ A Q 5 3 2
```

South is in 3NT on the ♡8 lead (high card lead from a poor suit). The defence needs to collect their tricks quickly. If East takes the ♡A and returns a heart, South makes twelve tricks. East needs the switch to spades, but if East plays the ♠J, the defence come to only two more tricks. South covers with the ♠Q. West wins and returns the suit to East's ♠K, but as South has the ♠9, the defence is over.

East cannot tell whether the ♠J or a low spade is best. In this case a low spade would give the defence four spade tricks and the ♠J only two.

Here is another case where you do not have dummy's high card exactly surrounded, but as with the jack in the earlier example, the ten can be the right card:

```
                North
                9 6 5
     West                    East
     Q 8 7                   K 10 3 2
                South
                A J 4
```

If East leads low, South ducks and makes two tricks. If East leads the ten, declarer can make only one trick. If South plays the jack, West wins and returns the eight. South has no answer.

When dummy has the eight, not the nine, the need can still exist for a surround play. Witness this deal from the Poland vs Italy match in the 1973 European Championships in Ostend:

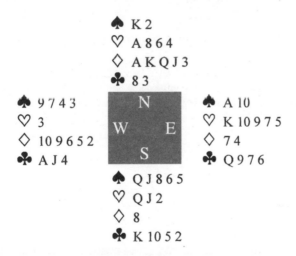

```
                ♠ K 2
                ♡ A 8 6 4
                ◇ A K Q J 3
                ♣ 8 3
  ♠ 9 7 4 3          N          ♠ A 10
  ♡ 3            W       E       ♡ K 10 9 7 5
  ◇ 10 9 6 5 2       S          ◇ 7 4
  ♣ A J 4                       ♣ Q 9 7 6
                ♠ Q J 8 6 5
                ♡ Q J 2
                ◇ 8
                ♣ K 10 5 2
```

Both Souths were in 3NT after East had bid hearts. Both Wests led the ♡3, ducked to the king. It was vital for East to switch to a club and Astolfi for Italy chose the ♣6. South ducked to dummy's ♣8. As the defence could not come to more than two club tricks, South made 3NT.

At the other table Andrzej Wilkosz recognised the surround position in clubs and switched to the ♣9. If South ducked this, another club would give the defence three clubs. When South played the ♣10, West won with the ♣J, cashed the ♣A and played a third club. That set up a club winner for East to take when in with the ♠A. Thus 3NT was one down.

Here are some other layouts for surround positions:

```
              North
              A 8 4
West                    East
J 3 2                   Q 9 7 6
              South
              K 10 5
```

East has dummy's eight surrounded. East should therefore lead the nine.

However, if dummy is similar and your holding is Q-J-x-x, you should normally lead low. For example:

```
              North
              A 8 4
West                    East
9 3 2                   Q J 7 6
              South
              K 10 5
```

If East leads the queen, South can win it with dummy's ace and finesse the ten later for three tricks. If East leads low, South has a guess whether to play low from hand or the ten. If South plays low, West's nine forces the ace and South makes two tricks only.

                    North
                    A 5 4
        West   East
        9 3 2   Q J 7 6
                    South
                    K 10 8

Likewise, if East leads the queen, South can make three tricks. If East leads low, South has a guess. If South inserts the eight, declarer makes two tricks only.

When you are sitting over declarer, you have to visualize the surround position. West intends to switch to this suit. Which card should West lead?

                    North
                    Q 4 3
        West
        K J 9

If declarer has the ace, declarer can make two tricks no matter which card you lead. If partner has A-10-x, then you can collect three tricks whatever you lead. Mind you, leading the nine would make it hard for partner to get it right.

The critical position is when partner has the ace and South the ten:

                    North
                    Q 4 3
        West   East
        K J 9   A 8 6 2
                    South
                    10 7 5

This is more difficult since West cannot see the card surrounded. To cater for this position, West should lead the jack. This gives the defence three tricks no matter how South plays.

This is similar:

```
                  North
                  A J 4
      West                    East
      Q 10 8 2                K 5 3
                  South
                  9 7 6
```

West cannot see South's cards, but if South has the king, South has three tricks regardless. If West leads low, dummy ducks and South can score two tricks.

West should lead the ten. This holds declarer to one trick when East has the king and South has the nine. The ten cannot cost in other layouts.

Likewise, West should lead the 10 here:

```
                  North
                  K J 4
      West                    East
      Q 10 8 2                A 5 3
                  South
                  9 7 6
```

If West leads low, South can duck in dummy and make two tricks. If West leads the ten, South is held to one trick, regardless of which card is played from dummy.

You can now test your defensive skills on this problem:

East dealer : Nil vulnerable

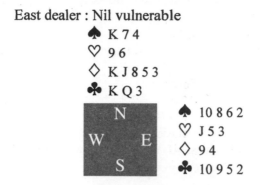

♠ K 7 4
♥ 9 6
♦ K J 8 5 3
♣ K Q 3

♠ 10 8 6 2
♥ J 5 3
♦ 9 4
♣ 10 9 5 2

West	North	East	South
		Pass	1NT (15-17)
2♥	3♣ (1)	Pass	3♦
Pass	3♥ (2)	Pass	4♥ (3)
Pass	5♦	All pass	

(1) Transfer, 5+ diamonds
(2) Asking for a stopper in hearts
(3) Cue-bid, agreeing diamonds

South supported the diamonds and suggested slam with the 4♥ cue-bid. North rejected the slam invitation.

West began with the ♥K. South took the ♥A and cashed the ♦A and the ♦K. West followed once and then threw the ♥2. Declarer continued with the ♣3 to the ace, club to the king and the ♣Q, partner following throughout. Declarer now calls for the ♥9. Your move?

Partner's ♥2 discard indicated six hearts originally. That means declarer's hand pattern is 3-2-5-3. As you can score only one trick in hearts, you clearly need two spade tricks to put the contract down. You must rise with the ♥J on the ♥9 and switch to a spade. Which one?

You cannot afford to play just any spade. You must shift to the
♠8, a surrounding play. This was the full deal:

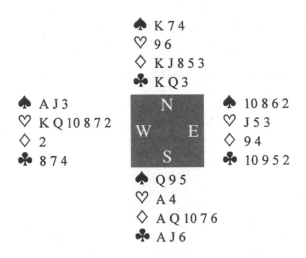

```
              ♠ K 7 4
              ♡ 9 6
              ◇ K J 8 5 3
              ♣ K Q 3
♠ A J 3              N              ♠ 10 8 6 2
♡ K Q 10 8 7 2                      ♡ J 5 3
◇ 2           W         E          ◇ 9 4
♣ 8 7 4              S              ♣ 10 9 5 2
              ♠ Q 9 5
              ♡ A 4
              ◇ A Q 10 7 6
              ♣ A J 6
```

If East switches to the ♠2 or the ♠6, South can play low in hand.
If West plays the ♠A, South has only one spade loser, of course,
but it does not help if West plays the ♠J. Dummy wins and South
can now play a low spade to the nine to lose just one spade trick.

The ♠10 will not work either. South can rise with the ♠Q. If
West ducks, South plays low to dummy's king. If West takes the
♠Q and returns the ♣3, South simply ducks in dummy and wins
with the ♠9.

The ♠8 is the only card that will do. If South plays low, so does
West. If South plays the ♠Q, West takes the ♠A and can afford
to return either spade. Finally, if South covers the ♠8 with the
♠9, West must co-operate by playing the ♠J. Dummy's ♠K
wins, but on the next spade from dummy East plays the ♠6 on the
♠4 or the ♠10 on the ♠8. This gives the defence two spade
tricks and takes 5◇ one down.

Chapter 6
Obligatory false cards

We play a false card when we know that declarer has guessed correctly in a suit and can take the maximum number of tricks. By playing a false card, we might just be able to divert declarer from the winning approach. This is a typical example:

1.

Declarer leads low to the jack (in all examples, dummy is North and declarer is South). It seems as though declarer will make four tricks. Lacking the ♠10 and ♠9, South will continue with the ♠A. When the ♠K falls, declarer makes all the tricks.

What if you play the ♠10 on the ♠J? This might persuade declarer that the layout is not as in #1, but as in #2:

2.   ♠ A J 8 x
              ♠ K x x   ♠ 10 9
                           ♠ Q x x x

If this is the situation, South needs to return to hand and lead the ♠Q in order to make four tricks by smothering the ♠9. If declarer does follow this line, then in layout #1, your ♠9 becomes a winner. Of course, playing the ♠10 will not always work, but it costs nothing to try. Sometimes it will succeed. If you follow with the lowest spade, South cannot go wrong. If you play the ♠9 or the ♠10, you give declarer a losing option.

3.   ♠ A J 9 x

         ♠ K x   ♠ 10 8 x

                          ♠ Q x x x

This is similar to #1 and #2. Declarer plays low to the jack,
intending to cash the ♠A next. If East drops the ♠8, South might
change tack, return to hand and lead the ♠Q, hoping to avoid a
loser when East has ♠10-8 doubleton.

To repeat: Whenever you are East with 10-x-x, always play the
middle card. The same applies to West. Consider this position:

4.   ♠ J x x

         ♠ 10 9 x   ♠ K x

                          ♠ A Q 8 x x

Declarer leads low from dummy to the queen. If West follows
with the lowest card, South will cash the ♠A next. If West plays
the ♠9 or ♠10, South might return to dummy and lead the ♠J,
thus creating a trick for West.

5.   ♠ A Q 9 2

         ♠ 10 8 6 5   ♠ K

                          ♠ J 7 4 3

Declarer leads low to the queen. If West plays the ♠5 or ♠6,
South will later play the ♠J and finesse the ♠9. Playing the ♠A
has no benefit, since if East started with K-10-8-x, South always
has a second loser.

West should play the ♠8 on the first round. That gives declarer a
choice to play either defender for the ♠10. South might play the
♠A to cater for the bare ♠8 with West and ♠K-10-x-x with East.

6.

♠ K J 7 2

♠ 6   ♠ A 10 8 3

♠ Q 9 5 4

South leads low to the ♠J. If East takes the ♠A, South will make three tricks. As in the previous example, East should play the ♠8. This might create an illusion that West began with ♠A-10-x-x and South might continue with a low spade to the queen. Now East collects two tricks.

7.   ♠ A K x x

♠ Q x   ♠ 10 9 x

♠ J 8 x x

Declarer cashes the ♠A. If both defenders play low, South will continue with the ♠K and make all the tricks. East should play the ♠9. Then South might play for this layout:

8.   ♠ A K x x

♠ Q x x   ♠ 10 9

♠ J 8 x x

If South crosses to hand and leads the ♠J, then East in #7 wins a trick. The defence is the same from the West seat:

9.   ♠ J 8 x x

♠ 10 9 x   ♠ Q x

♠ A K x x

When South plays low to the ace, West must drop the ♠9 or ♠10.

10.   ♠ x

  ♠ J 10 x   ♠ A x

          ♠ K Q 9 x x x x

Declarer leads low from dummy to the ♠K or ♠Q. If West plays
low, South has no option but to continue with a low card and hope
the ace is doubleton. If West follows with the ♠10, then declarer
might be duped into thinking the layout looks like this:

11.   ♠ x

    ♠ J 10   ♠ A x x

          ♠ K Q 9 x x x x

In this case, playing the other top honour is the winning move, but
if declarer does that, the defence score two tricks in #10.

What if we swap the East and West holdings:

12.   ♠ K Q 9 x x x x

    ♠ A x   ♠ J 10 x

          ♠ x

13.   ♠ - - -

    ♠ J 10 x   ♠ K x

          ♠ A Q 9 x x x x x

In #12 South plays low to the king; in #13, South cashes the ♠A.
If the defender with J-10-x plays low, declarer has no real choice.
If the ♠10 is played, South might go wrong.

Here the focus is on East:

14.

♠ A Q 9 x x x x x

♠ K x   ♠ J 10 x

♠ - - -

Declarer plays the ♠A. If East follows low, declarer will continue with a low spade and lose only one trick.

15.   ♠ Q 8 x x

♠ x   ♠ J 9 x x

♠ A K 10 x

Declarer starts with the ♠A. If East follows low, declarer will no doubt play low to the queen next and then finesse the ♠10. To play the ♠K on the second round is of no avail. If West began with ♠J-9-x-x, South cannot avoid losing a trick.

If East plays the ♠9, declarer might misread the position. If South takes the ♠9 as a possible singleton, South will play the ♠K next and then East collects a trick.

Declarer does better by playing the first round from dummy towards the A-K in hand. East will hardly play the ♠9 now in case West began with the ♠10 bare.

16.   ♠ A Q x

♠ x   ♠ K 10 8 x

♠ J 9 7 x x

Declarer plays low to the queen. If East takes the ♠K, South will cash the ♠A next and take the rest of the tricks. What if East plays the ♠8 under the ♠Q? Might declarer not play for this:

17.   ♠ A Q x

          ♠ K 10 x x   ♠ 8

                      ♠ J 9 7 x x

After a low spade to the queen and East's ♠8, South cannot afford to cash the ♠A. That gives West two tricks. Perhaps South will return to hand and lead the ♠J. That also caters for East holding ♠10-8 originally. How disappointed South will be when it is really layout #16 and East collects two tricks.

In the next position playing the eight cannot hurt and might help:

18.   ♠ K J
                          ♡ K 4
                          ◇ A K 6 5 4
                          ♣ K J 3 2

    ♠ Q 10 8 5   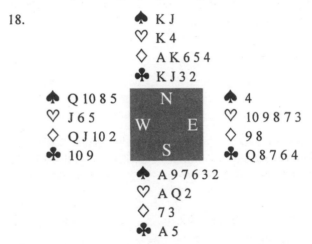   ♠ 4
    ♡ J 6 5   ♡ 10 9 8 7 3
    ◇ Q J 10 2   ◇ 9 8
    ♣ 10 9   ♣ Q 8 7 6 4

                          ♠ A 9 7 6 3 2
                          ♡ A Q 2
                          ◇ 7 3
                          ♣ A 5

South is in 6♠ on the lead of the ◇Q. The play seems simple enough. South takes the ◇Q in dummy, comes to hand with a club and plays a low spade to dummy's jack and twelve tricks.

Suppose West plays the ♠8 on the first spade. If the ♠8 is singleton, the required safety play is to rise with the ♠K and lead the ♠J, catering for East's ♠Q-10-5-4. This risks only an overtrick if West began ♠Q-10-8. Alas, the safety play in the actual layout is a disaster! (We trust that this will not deter any readers from the safety play. You just have to congratulate West on fine defence.)

19.   ♠ A Q 10 7 x

    ♠ K x x   ♠ 9 8 x x

           ♠ J

Playing in no-trumps, with only one outside entry to dummy, South leads the ♠J and overtakes with the ♠Q. Next comes the ♠A and finally a low spade, if East has followed low both times. With the ♠K falling on the third round, dummy's ♠10-7 is worth two more tricks.

East should follow with the ♠8 on the second round to create an illusion that the layout is like this:

20.   ♠ A Q 10 7 x

    ♠ K x x x   ♠ 9 8 x

           ♠ J

If declarer takes the bait in and plays the ♠10 on the third round in #19, the defence will collect two tricks and declarer makes only two spade tricks in all when dummy has only one outside entry

21.   ♠ K J 8 7 x

    ♠ Q x x   ♠ 10 9 x

           ♠ A x

If declarer needs five tricks, then there is no hope for the defence. South will surely cash the ♠A and finesse the ♠J. If declarer needs only four tricks, you might be able seduce him into a safety play by dropping the ♠9 on the first round. This could suggest one of the following layouts and give the defence a trick that was otherwise not forthcoming:

22.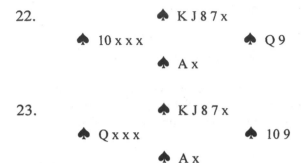

♠ K J 8 7 x

♠ 10 x x x   ♠ Q 9

♠ A x

23.   ♠ K J 8 7 x

♠ Q x x x   ♠ 10 9

♠ A x

If East drops the ♠9 on the first round, South cannot afford to finesse the ♠J next, because in #22 that would mean two spade losers and leave South with only three tricks. The safety play is to cash the ♠K. Now West scores a trick in #21.

Also, with 9-x or 10-x doubleton, East should play the top card, suggesting a holding of 10-9, Q-9 or Q-10. That might persuade South to cash the ♠K on the second round. If so, West can collect two tricks and declarer makes only three.

24.   North
                    ♠ K 8 7 3 2

                    South
                    ♠ A Q

South is in no-trumps and needs four tricks for success. Dummy has only one outside entry. If East has 9-x, 10-x, J-x or 10-9-x, J-9-x, J-10-x or J-10-9-x, then in every case East should play a high card on the first round. South might now place East with 10-9, J-9 or J-10 doubleton. If so, South's best chance is to overtake the queen. East's play will thus hold South to two tricks. If East lazily follows low on the ace, then the best chance for declarer is to cash the queen, cross to dummy and cash the king. That costs the defence a trick.

25.

It looks as though the defence has no hope for a trick here, but what if West plays the ♠10 or the ♠J when South leads low to the ♠Q? That might persuade South to finesse the ♠9 next.

26.

The standard safety play here is to cash the ♠A, followed by the low spade to dummy's ♠10 to guard against this specific layout. What if East plays the ♠9 on the first round? Now declarer must consider the possibility that either of these positions exist:

27.

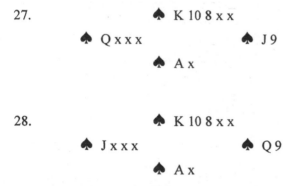

28.

In each case, finessing the ♠10 will result in losing two tricks. The winning play in #27 and #28 is ♠A, followed by the ♠K. If East has played the ♠9 in #26, declarer is very likely to continue with a spade to the king. If so, the defence comes to two tricks and another false card has done its work.

29.   ♠ A 10 7 6 2

  ♠ K J 5 4   ♠ 8 3

           ♠ Q 9

South plays the ♠Q and West and North both follow low. If East has played the ♠3, South will see merit in continuing with the ♠9 and letting it run if West plays low. Of course, if West covers the ♠Q or the ♠9, declarer loses only one trick. If East contributes the ♠8 on the first round, South will take into account ♠J-8 with East and might continue with the ♠9 to the ♠A.

This deal occurred in the Denmark vs Poland match at the 1989 European Championships in Turku, Finland. The hero is Poland's Marek Szymanowski.

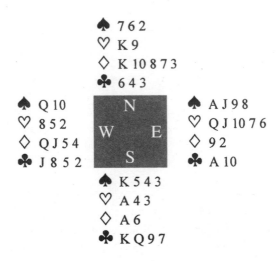

           ♠ 7 6 2
           ♡ K 9
           ◇ K 10 8 7 3
           ♣ 6 4 3

♠ Q 10   N   ♠ A J 9 8
♡ 8 5 2   ♡ Q J 10 7 6
◇ Q J 5 4   W   E   ◇ 9 2
♣ J 8 5 2   S   ♣ A 10

           ♠ K 5 4 3
           ♡ A 4 3
           ◇ A 6
           ♣ K Q 9 7

South was in 1NT on the ♡5 lead to the ♡A. South played the ◇A and Szymanowski, East, followed with the ◇9. South continued with the ◇6 to the ◇K and went one down.

30.

Declarer has a 50% chance to lose only one trick by cashing the ♠A, followed by a low card and a correct guess. How can we reduce South's odds? If East plays low, the odds stay at 50%, but what if East plays the ♠9 on the ♠A? Now South has to take into account that the layout in #31 or in #32 might exist:

31.

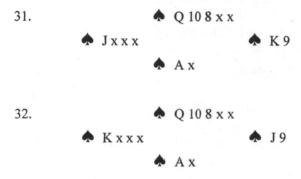

In #31 South has two losers whether the ♠Q or a low card is played from dummy on the second round. In #32, finessing the ♠10 leads to two losers, but rising with the ♠Q will hold the losers to one.

Playing the ♠Q on the second rounds wins whenever West began with ♠K-x-x or ♠K-x-x-x. It is clear that if East plays the ♠9 on the first round in #30, that this will almost always convince South to play low to the ♠Q on the second round with the pleasing result of two tricks for the defence.

33.

♠ A K x x x

♠ Q 10   ♠ x x x

♠ J 9 x

When declarer plays low towards dummy, West can see that he has no trick in this suit. Why not follow with the ♠Q on the first round? It cannot cost and it might gain a trick. A comparable position existed on this deal from the 1971 Far East Open Pairs:

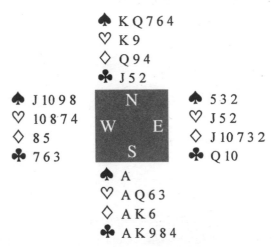

♠ K Q 7 6 4
♡ K 9
◇ Q 9 4
♣ J 5 2

♠ J 10 9 8   ♠ 5 3 2
♡ 10 8 7 4   ♡ J 5 2
◇ 8 5   ◇ J 10 7 3 2
♣ 7 6 3   ♣ Q 10

♠ A
♡ A Q 6 3
◇ A K 6
♣ A K 9 8 4

South reached 7♣ and West led the ♠J. South won and played the ♣A: low – low – queen! Who can blame South for continuing with the ♣9 and letting it run? East was Ron Klinger of Australia.

34.

♠ A Q x x x

♠ K 10   ♠ x x x

♠ J 9 x

This position is analogous to the previous example. When declarer leads low towards dummy, West's play of the ♠K might convince declarer to finesse the ♠9 on the way back.

The principle applies identically when East has the critical cards:

35.   ♠ J 9 x

♠ x x x   ♠ K 10 (♠ Q 10)

                            ♠ A Q x x x (♠ A K x x x)

When declarer leads low from dummy, East should play the top honour in each case. It also applies to this position when declarer has only one chance to finesse and leads low towards dummy:

36.   ♠ A Q

♠ K 10   ♠ x x x

                            ♠ J 9 x x x x

As the king is doomed anyway, you might as well play it. This arose in the famous final of the 1975 Bermuda Bowl:

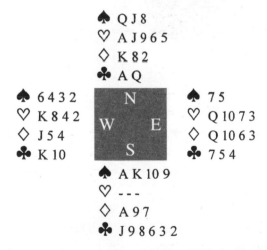

                ♠ Q J 8
                ♡ A J 9 6 5
                ◇ K 8 2
                ♣ A Q

♠ 6 4 3 2   ♠ 7 5
♡ K 8 4 2   ♡ Q 10 7 3
◇ J 5 4   ◇ Q 10 6 3
♣ K 10   ♣ 7 5 4

                ♠ A K 10 9
                ♡ - - -
                ◇ A 9 7
                ♣ J 9 8 6 3 2

With four boards to go after this one, Italy led by 12 Imps. In the Closed Room the USA made 6NT by North on the ♣5 lead. Italy made 7♣ via the club finesse and the ♣K falling.

The lead was a heart, ruffed by South to lead a trump. Suppose Eddie Kantar, West, had played the ♣K. Giorgio Belladonna would now place East with ♣10-7-5-4 and play accordingly to produce a trump coup, in the hope that East began with at least three spades. He would discard a diamond on the ♡A, ruff another heart, cash the ◇A, ◇K, followed by the ♠Q, ♠J and a spade to the king. This is the ending South would aim to reach:

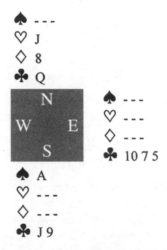

```
        ♠ - - -
        ♡ J
        ◇ 8
        ♣ Q
                        ♠ - - -
    N                   ♡ - - -
 W     E                ◇ - - -
    S                   ♣ 10 7 5
        ♠ A
        ♡ - - -
        ◇ - - -
        ♣ J 9
```

If so, South would ruff the ♠A with the ♣Q, leaving the ♣J-9 poised over East's ♣10-7 at trick 12. On the actual layout, the third spade would be ruffed by East and the USA would have won 17 Imps instead of losing 12. That would have made them winners of the World Championship by 3 Imps.

The situation is equivalent when East has Q-9 or K-9:

37.   ♠ 10 8 x

                                ♠ Q 9 (♠K 9)

When dummy leads low, East should play the honour.

A well-timed false card can easily mislead declarer. Here is a fine example from Wally Malaczynski, formerly of Poland, now living in Australia:

Dealer South : North-South vulnerable

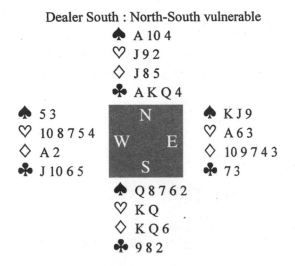

♠ A 10 4
♥ J 9 2
♦ J 8 5
♣ A K Q 4

♠ 5 3
♥ 10 8 7 5 4
♦ A 2
♣ J 10 6 5

♠ K J 9
♥ A 6 3
♦ 10 9 7 4 3
♣ 7 3

♠ Q 8 7 6 2
♥ K Q
♦ K Q 6
♣ 9 8 2

South reached 4♠ and West began with the ♦A and the ♦2. South won and, naturally fearing a diamond ruff, wanted to remove as many trumps as possible. When he played the ♠2 to the ace, Malaczynski dropped the ♠K! Notice that this does not cost a trick, no matter who has the ♠Q.

To South is appeared that West must have started with ♠J-9-5-3. If so, it was essential to come to hand to lead low towards dummy's ♠10-4. Declarer played a heart from dummy. East rose with the ace and gave West a diamond ruff. East still had a trump trick to come and so the contract was defeated.

You can see what would happen if East had played the ♠9 under the ♠A at trick 3. Declarer would simply play another spade and the defence would collect only one spade and two red aces.

Malaczynski was also the defensive hero on this deal:

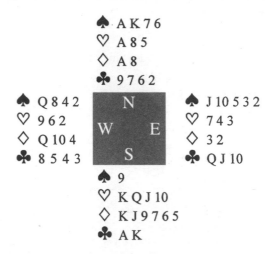

♠ A K 7 6
♡ A 8 5
◇ A 8
♣ 9 7 6 2

♠ Q 8 4 2
♡ 9 6 2
◇ Q 10 4
♣ 8 5 4 3

♠ J 10 5 3 2
♡ 7 4 3
◇ 3 2
♣ Q J 10

♠ 9
♡ K Q J 10
◇ K J 9 7 6 5
♣ A K

North-South had found their way to 7♡. This is a fair grand slam, respectable only because the trumps are so strong. West led a trump and on normal play declarer has an easy time: draw a second round of trumps, leaving the ace in dummy, and then play ◇A, ◇K and a third diamond, ruffed with the ♡A. A club to hand allows you to draw the missing trumps and claim thirteen tricks.

That was declarer's plan, but Malaczynski found a way to divert declarer from the winning path. South won the trump lead in hand and cashed another heart. On the low diamond at trick 3, West played the ◇Q!

Clearly expecting this to be a singleton, South could not afford to play another diamond, lest West ruff. Therefore South cashed the ♡A, to which all followed. (If not, South could come to hand with a club, draw the missing trump and return to dummy with a spade.) It was routine to continue with a diamond and finesse the ◇9. Alas, things are not always what they seem and when West won with the ◇10, another contract had bit the dust.

38.
♠ 10 8 x

♠ K x x   ♠ Q 9

♠ A J x x x

Declarer leads low from dummy. If East plays the ♠9, South will lose the ♠J to the ♠K, but will cash the ♠A next. If East plays the ♠Q on the first round, there is a distinct chance that South will finesse the ♠8 later to guard against this layout:

39.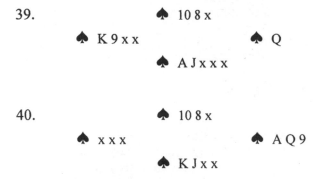
♠ 10 8 x

♠ K 9 x x   ♠ Q

♠ A J x x x

40.
♠ 10 8 x

♠ x x x   ♠ A Q 9

♠ K J x x

With the cards lying so well for declarer, it looks like we can make only the ♠A. Declarer will lead low from dummy to the jack and next time low from dummy to the king. At least that is the theory. What will happen in practice if East plays the ♠Q on the first round? Declarer will no doubt 'see' a different layout:

41.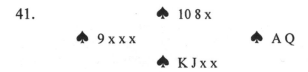
♠ 10 8 x

♠ 9 x x x   ♠ A Q

♠ K J x x

After capturing the ♠Q, South will continue with a low spade and finesse the ♠8. Bingo! Now the defenders have two spade tricks instead of just one.

Here is a slightly different theme from the Polish Teams Trials:

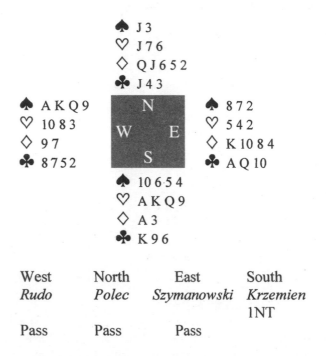

```
                    ♠ J 3
                    ♡ J 7 6
                    ◇ Q J 6 5 2
                    ♣ J 4 3
♠ A K Q 9              N              ♠ 8 7 2
♡ 10 8 3         W         E         ♡ 5 4 2
◇ 9 7                                ◇ K 10 8 4
♣ 8 7 5 2              S              ♣ A Q 10
                    ♠ 10 6 5 4
                    ♡ A K Q 9
                    ◇ A 3
                    ♣ K 9 6
```

West	North	East	South
Rudo	*Polec*	*Szymanowski*	*Krzemien*
			1NT
Pass	Pass	Pass	

Krzemien reminisces:

'West led the ♠K, ♠Q and switched to the ♣7, low from dummy and East contributed the ♣10. I won, crossed to dummy via the ♡J and led the ◇Q. When that held the trick, I had my 1NT contract. I have to admit that if Szymanowski, East, had played the ♣Q instead of the ♣10, I would have placed the ♣10 with Rudo, West. No longer concerned about losing three club tricks, since the ♣9-x opposite the ♣J-x now creates a stopper if West does have the ♣10, I would have played ◇A and another diamond. That would have meant one down, as the defence can now come to four spades, a diamond and two clubs.'

Now we come to the combination that gives us the best prospects for successful deception, those involving the J-9.

42.

Remember #30-32? When South starts with the ♠A, playing the ♠9 is likely to persuade declarer to lead to the ♠Q on the next round and smother our jack. What happens if we play the ♠J under the ♠A? Declarer will almost certainly duck the second round completely, counting on this layout:

43.

What if we change the setting slightly:

44.

If East plays the ♠9 under the ♠K, South will play the ♠A next, hoping for honour-nine with East. That gives East-West only one trick. Suppose East plays the ♠J on the ♠K? What will declarer do now? If declarer plays to the ace and finds East with ♠Q-J bare, there is still a trick to be lost to West's ♠9-x-x-x. South might therefore finesse the ♠8 on the second round. If East did start with ♠Q-J bare, declarer loses a trick anyway, but finessing the ♠8 might help declarer later in the play if East's ♠J happened to be singleton. If declarer does finesse the ♠8 the defence comes to two tricks. Mission accomplished.

45.   ♠ Q x

♠ J 9   ♠ K x x

                          ♠ A 10 8 x x x

South leads low towards the ♠Q. If West follows with the ♠9, South might cash the ♠A next, but if West plays the ♠J on the first round, South will almost certainly finesse the ♠8 later.

46.   ♠ 10 8 x

  ♠ K x x   ♠ J 9

                          ♠ A Q x x x

South leads low from dummy. If West plays the ♠J, the ♠Q loses to the ♠K, but South is sure to finesse the ♠8 next.

47.   ♠ 10 8 x

  ♠ A x x   ♠ J 9

                          ♠ K Q x x x

Same story. South leads low from dummy. East follows with the ♠J and almost always gains a trick with the ♠9.

48.   ♠ K 8 x

  ♠ A x x   ♠ J 9

                          ♠ Q 10 x x x

South leads low from dummy. The play of the ♠J cannot hurt.

49.   ♠ Q 8 x

  ♠ x x x   ♠ K J 9

                          ♠ A 10 x x

Declarer plays low from dummy. If East follows with the ♠9, South will put in the ♠10 and the defence makes only one trick.

If East follows with the ♠J on the first round, South will surely take the ♠A and, counting on West to have started with ♠9-x-x-x, finesse the 8 on the way back.

50.

Here, too, if South leads low and West plays the ♠9, declarer will make three tricks. If West plays the ♠J, declarer will win with the ♠Q and is bound to duck from both hands on the next round, playing West to have started with ♠A-J tight.

51.

The situation looks hopeless for the defence to score more than one trick, but what if East plays the ♠J when a low spade is led from the North hand? South will probably finesse the ♠8 next.

52.

To lose only two on this layout, South should lead low from dummy and play low if East follows with the ♠9. South hopes the suit is 2-2 or West began with a singleton ace or king. If East plays the ♠J, South will almost certainly cover with the ♠Q in case the ♠J is singleton or East began with ♠A-K-J. Once South plays the ♠Q on the actual layout the defence has three tricks.

53.   ♠ K 8 4 3 2

♠ QJ9   ♠ A

♠ 10 7 6 5

Able to afford two losers, but not three, South leads low from hand.
If West plays the ♠9, South will duck in dummy as a safety play.
When the ♠A falls, South has achieved his aim. If the ♠A has
not fallen, South later leads from hand again. What if West plays
the ♠J or ♠Q on the first round? Now South must cover with the
♠K, lest West began with a singleton honour, and the defence
collect three tricks.

54.   ♠ K 4

♠ QJ9   ♠ A 8 6

♠ 10 7 5 3 2

This layout also calls for West to play an honour: If South leads
low and West plays the ♠9, East might duck North's ♠K for fear
that the actual layout looks like this and to mislead declarer as to
the location of the honours:

55.   ♠ K 4

♠ J 9   ♠ A 8 6

♠ Q 10 7 5 3 2

Therefore West *must* play an honour in #54 to prevent East from
doing the wrong thing.

56.   ♠ K J 9 2

♠ Q 8 5   ♠ 10 6 3

♠ A 7 4

If South plays the ace, East should play the ♠10 to tempt South
to play East for ♠Q-10 bare.

Even if South leads low to the ♣J, East should play the ♣10 to convince South to finesse again by returning to hand with the ace. Sometimes that might produce a profit.

57.

♠ A Q 10 3 2

♠ K 5   ♠ J 6

♠ 9 8 7 4

South finesses the queen. If South is known to have four cards in the suit, East should follow with the jack.

Here is Fred Karpin, USA expert, in action:

NORTH ♠ A K J 3 ♡ K Q ◇ 5 3 ♣ 9 7 5 3 2 WEST EAST ♠ 9 8 5 4 2 ♠ Q 10 7 6 ♡ 3 ♡ 8 7 5 4 2 ◇ Q J 8 4 2 ◇ A 6 ♣ J 6 ♣ K 4 SOUTH ♠ - - - ♡ A J 10 9 6 ◇ K 10 9 7 ♣ A Q 10 8	West North East South 1♡ Pass 1♠ Pass 2♣ Pass 4♣ Pass 4◇ Pass 4♡ Pass 6♣ Pass Pass Pass West led the ◇Q. East took the ◇A and returned the ◇6. South won, crossed to a heart in dummy and finessed the queen of clubs. When Karpin followed with the jack of clubs, declarer tried to reach dummy with a heart to repeat the club finesse. No luck there! Karpin ruffed. One down. If West had played low on the first round of trumps, South would have played the ♣A next.

58.   North
                       ♠ A Q 9 8
       West   East
       ♠ K 2   ♠ 10 3
                       South
                       ♠ J 7 6 5 4

When South finesses the queen, East should drop the ten.

59.   North
                       ♠ Q 10 5 4
       West   East
       ♠ K 8 2   ♠ J 9 3
                       South
                       ♠ A 7 6

When South cashes the ace and plays low to the queen, East should drop the jack. It might not gain East anything, but it might cause South to use up a vital entry.

60.   North
                       ♠ K J 8 4 3 2
       West   East
       ♠ A 10   ♠ Q 9
                       South
                       ♠ 7 6 5

If South plays low to the king, East should drop the queen. West's ten tells East the layout of the suit.

61.   North
                       ♠ A K 10 2
       West   East
       ♠ Q 9 7   ♠ J 8 3
                       South
                       ♠ 6 5 4

If South cashes the ace and king, East should play three, then jack.

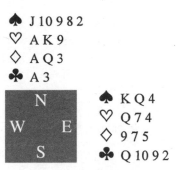

♠ J 10 9 8 2
♡ A K 9
◇ A Q 3
♣ A 3

♠ K Q 4
♡ Q 7 4
◇ 9 7 5
♣ Q 10 9 2

South opens 1♠ and North-South end in 6♠. West leads the ♡J, ♡A from dummy. Which card do you play?

With a 'surprise' in trumps, we might be able to lure declarer into a mistake. Here is how USA representative Gail Greenberg did it:

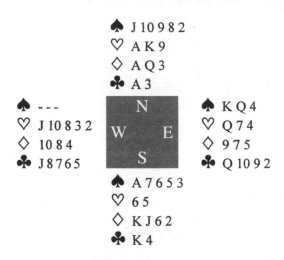

♠ J 10 9 8 2
♡ A K 9
◇ A Q 3
♣ A 3

♠ - - -
♡ J 10 8 3 2
◇ 10 8 4
♣ J 8 7 6 5

♠ K Q 4
♡ Q 7 4
◇ 9 7 5
♣ Q 10 9 2

♠ A 7 6 5 3
♡ 6 5
◇ K J 6 2
♣ K 4

On the ♡A from dummy, Greenberg dropped the ♡Q. The usual safety play is to take a first-round spade finesse, but South could not risk that, lest West win and give East a heart ruff. When South continued with a spade to the ace, the slam was one off.

And now something for the fans of match-points:

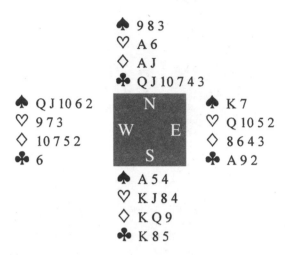

♠ 9 8 3
♡ A 6
◇ A J
♣ Q J 10 7 4 3

♠ Q J 10 6 2
♡ 9 7 3
◇ 10 7 5 2
♣ 6

♠ K 7
♡ Q 10 5 2
◇ 8 6 4 3
♣ A 9 2

♠ A 5 4
♡ K J 8 4
◇ K Q 9
♣ K 8 5

South opened 1NT (15-17) and ended in 3NT on the ♠Q lead. Which spade should East play?

Recommended is for East to play low. This suggests a 3-card holding and declarer is now likely to duck twice. If so, we will have 'stolen' a trick. Overtaking with the ♠K here has no merit, as East can tell from the points revealed that West has no entry.

The corollary is that with ♠K-x-x, East should overtake and return the suit, suggesting king-doubleton. If South falls into the trap and takes the second spade, the defence scores an extra trick.

We end this chapter with a fine piece of defence by Martin Hoffman:

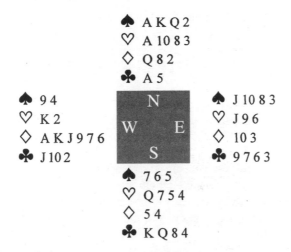

♠ A K Q 2
♥ A 10 8 3
♦ Q 8 2
♣ A 5

♠ 9 4   ♠ J 10 8 3
♥ K 2   ♥ J 9 6
♦ A K J 9 7 6   ♦ 10 3
♣ J 10 2   ♣ 9 7 6 3

♠ 7 6 5
♥ Q 7 5 4
♦ 5 4
♣ K Q 8 4

After West opened 1♦ and North doubled, South ended in 4♥. West began with the ♦A, followed by the ♦K and a switch to the ♣J. Declarer took the ♣A and continued with the ♦Q to tempt East to ruff and so simplify the trump play for South. However, East discarded a club on the ♦Q and so South had to start the trump suit himself.

How could East tell not to ruff the ♦Q? Because West would have played a third diamond if a ruff was feasible.

The bidding told South that the ♥K was with West, but how many hearts did West hold? Declarer cashed the ♥A, followed by the ♥3. Hoffman followed with ♥6, then ♥J!

To South it was obvious that West had started with ♥K-9-2 and so he covered the ♥J with the ♥Q. West took the ♥K and now played a fourth diamond. This promoted East's ♥9 to defeat the contract.

If Hoffman had routinely followed ♥6, then ♥9 on the first two rounds of trumps, declarer would almost certainly have played low on the second heart in the hope of finding ♥K-2 with West. When that did occur, South would have made the contract.

Chapter 7
Suit-preference signals

Average players love to use suit-preference signals frequently and everywhere. They are on the lookout for any help they can get and a suspiciously low card or high card from partner is like a beacon.

By contrast advanced players use suit-preference signals sparingly. Encourage/discourage and count signals are usually enough to find a way to defeat a contract. Still, there are situations where a suit-preference signal is mandatory. We can try to classify these suit-preference positions.

1. Partner has shown a 5+ suit and you lead a card that will keep you on lead for trick 2.

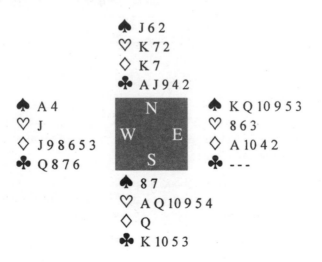

East opened 2♠, weak, and South has reached 4♡. You, West, lead the ♠A and we suggest the following options for East:

- ♠3 (lowest card) = suit-preference for clubs, the lowest suit
- ♠9 (middle card) = encouraging a spade continuation
- ♠Q (high card) = suit-preference for diamonds, the higher suit

If you play the ♠K, partner takes that as showing ♠K-Q-10.

The best play by East on the preceding deal is the ♠3 to ask partner to lead a club.

Suit-preference signals are also known as McKenney or Lavinthal signals. This example comes from *Defence Strategy in Bridge* by Hy Lavinthal:

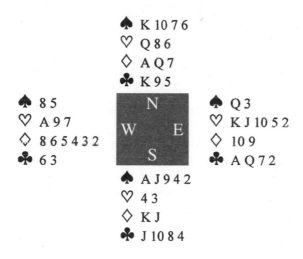

```
                    ♠ K 10 7 6
                    ♡ Q 8 6
                    ◇ A Q 7
                    ♣ K 9 5
   ♠ 8 5              N            ♠ Q 3
   ♡ A 9 7                         ♡ K J 10 5 2
   ◇ 8 6 5 4 3 2   W     E         ◇ 10 9
   ♣ 6 3                           ♣ A Q 7 2
                     S
                    ♠ A J 9 4 2
                    ♡ 4 3
                    ◇ K J
                    ♣ J 10 8 4
```

North opened 1♣, East overcalled 1♡ and South ended in 4♠. West began with the ♡A. Which card should East play?

According to Lavinthal, even a 5-card suit enables the defence to use a suit-preference card at trick 1. If you and your partner(s) agree with that, East should follow with the ♡2 here to ask for a club switch. A club switch takes 4♠ two down, while a second heart allows South to escape for one off.

Here is another interesting example of partnership agreements dealing with suit-preference:

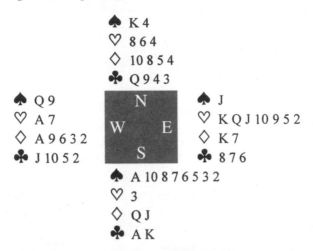

```
                    ♠ K 4
                    ♡ 8 6 4
                    ◇ 10 8 5 4
                    ♣ Q 9 4 3
    ♠ Q 9                         ♠ J
    ♡ A 7          N              ♡ K Q J 10 9 5 2
    ◇ A 9 6 3 2  W   E            ◇ K 7
    ♣ J 10 5 2     S              ♣ 8 7 6
                    ♠ A 10 8 7 6 5 3 2
                    ♡ 3
                    ◇ Q J
                    ♣ A K
```

East opened 3♡ and South bid 4♠, passed out. West led the ♡A and East played the ♡K (or ♡Q, if that is your approach) as a suit-preference signal to show strength in the higher outside suit, namely diamonds. The trump suit is excluded. West now led the ◇2 to show an honour in diamonds and asking partner to return a diamond. If West had the ♡A singleton, the switch would have been to the ◇9, showing no desire for a diamond return and thus suggesting a return to hearts for an eventual trump promotion. That would produce a successful defence if declarer held:

$$\spadesuit \text{ A } 10\,8\,7\,6\,5\,3\,2 \quad \heartsuit \text{ 7 3} \quad \diamondsuit \text{ Q} \quad \clubsuit \text{ A K}$$

On the actual layout, East took the ◇K and returned a diamond to West's ace. The next diamond was ruffed by East with the ♠J, an uppercut creating a trump trick for the defenders.

What if declarer's hand looked like this:

$$\spadesuit \text{ A Q } 10\,8\,6\,5\,2 \quad \heartsuit \text{ 7 3} \quad \diamondsuit \text{ 8 5} \quad \clubsuit \text{ A K}$$

Now West, with no hope of a trump promotion, should switch to the ◊A at trick 2 and continue with a low diamond. East wins and cashes a heart winner or gives West a heart ruff.

Finally, suppose West has only four diamonds and declarer holds these cards:

♠ A Q 10 8 6 5 2   ♡ 7   ◊ Q J 6   ♣ A K

West plays the ◊2 at trick 2, requesting a diamond return, and can give East a ruff with the third round of diamonds.

These variations demonstrate how we can sometimes inform partner precisely how we feel the defence should go to find the precise path to defeat the contract. Therefore you cannot afford to play automatic count signals, but need to gear the signalling to the actual layout to find the successful defence.

This kind of defence requires both partners to have considerable bridge knowledge as well as good imagination to perceive the possibilities to find the winning defence. Neither novices nor intermediate players will want to include these methods and signals directly into their agreements. That is mainly because their knowledge is not sufficient yet.

The aim is to illustrate the vast possibilities in defensive play and ask players to keep working on their bridge skills. With ambition and dedication there is no limit to the success you can achieve when defending. The day will come when you and your equally ambitious partner will be able to implement these ideas and move to a higher and more successful level.

2. You lead a suit bid or supported by partner and it turns out that this sets up tricks for declarer.

Dealer West : North-South vulnerable

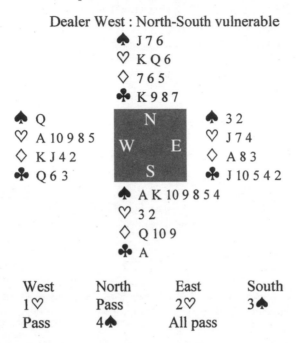

```
                    ♠ J 7 6
                    ♡ K Q 6
                    ◇ 7 6 5
                    ♣ K 9 8 7
  ♠ Q                   N              ♠ 3 2
  ♡ A 10 9 8 5      W       E         ♡ J 7 4
  ◇ K J 4 2                           ◇ A 8 3
  ♣ Q 6 3              S              ♣ J 10 5 4 2
                    ♠ A K 10 9 8 5 4
                    ♡ 3 2
                    ◇ Q 10 9
                    ♣ A
```

West	North	East	South
1♡	Pass	2♡	3♠
Pass	4♠	All pass	

West leads the ♡A. There is no point East giving West count or an encourage/discourage signal. It is obvious that West must switch, but to which suit? East should play the ♡J to show strength in diamonds. West shifts to the ◇2 and the defence takes three diamond tricks.

If East had ♣A-J-10 and declarer's hand looked like this:

♠ A K 10 9 8 5 4   ♡ 3   ◇ A Q   ♣ 6 5 4

East plays the ♡2 at trick 1 and West switches to the ♣Q to collect three club tricks.

NORTH
- ♠ K Q 7
- ♡ Q 4 3 2
- ♢ J 7 6
- ♣ J 3 2

WEST
- ♠ 3
- ♡ A 7
- ♢ 10 9 4 3 2
- ♣ K 7 6 5 4

EAST
- ♠ 10 9 8 4 2
- ♡ 9 8
- ♢ K 8 5
- ♣ A 10 9

SOUTH
- ♠ A J 6 5
- ♡ K J 10 6 5
- ♢ A Q
- ♣ Q 8

3. When partner leads an obvious or almost certain singleton and dummy or declarer wins the trick.

West	North	East	South
			1♡
Pass	2♡	Pass	2♠
Pass	4♡	All pass	

West leads the ♠3. No matter which card is played from dummy, East should play the ♠2 to show an entry in the low suit, clubs.

Dealer South : Both vulnerable

NORTH
- ♠ Q 7 6
- ♡ K J 7 6 2
- ♢ 6
- ♣ J 7 6 5

WEST
- ♠ A K 9 8 2
- ♡ A
- ♢ Q 10 8 7
- ♣ Q 3 2

EAST
- ♠ J 10 5 4
- ♡ 10 5 3
- ♢ J 9 5 4 3
- ♣ K

SOUTH
- ♠ 3
- ♡ Q 9 8 4
- ♢ A K 2
- ♣ A 10 9 8 4

4. When the layout of the suit led by declarer or the defence is known.

West	North	East	South
			1♣
1♠	Dble	3♠	4♡
Pass	Pass	Pass	

West leads the ♠A. East plays the ♠4, neither count (as East must have four spades for the jump to 3♠) nor attitude. As the spade position is known, the ♠4 is suit-preference for clubs. A club switch at trick 2 can lead to the defeat of 4♡.

Dealer South : Nil vulnerable

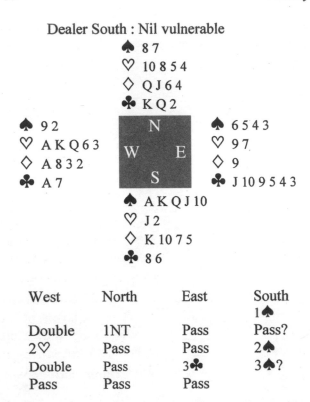

                ♠ 8 7
                ♡ 10 8 5 4
                ◇ Q J 6 4
                ♣ K Q 2

♠ 9 2   ♠ 6 5 4 3
♡ A K Q 6 3   ♡ 9 7
◇ A 8 3 2   ◇ 9
♣ A 7   ♣ J 10 9 5 4 3

                ♠ A K Q J 10
                ♡ J 2
                ◇ K 10 7 5
                ♣ 8 6

West	North	East	South
			1♠
Double	1NT	Pass	Pass?
2♡	Pass	Pass	2♠
Double	Pass	3♣	3♠?
Pass	Pass	Pass	

West, Tomasz Przybora, began with the ♡A and the ♡K. East, Krzysztof Martens had expected a heart continuation at trick 2, since he had denied three hearts, and deliberately followed with the ♡9, then ♡7, even though this showed an odd number of hearts in their methods.

As this was false count (East-West play low-high with an even number) the signal was taken as suit-preference, high first for the higher suit, diamonds. West switched to the ◇A, followed by the ◇2, suit-preference for clubs. A club to the ace and another diamond took the contract two down.

5. Dummy turns up with a singleton in the suit you have led and it is not logical to continue that suit.

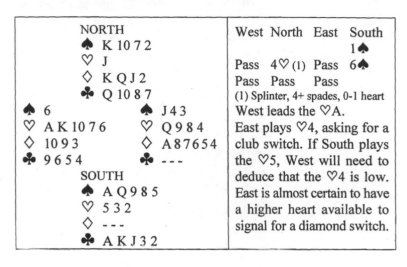

NORTH
♠ K 10 7 2
♡ J
♢ K Q J 2
♣ Q 10 8 7

♠ 6   ♠ J 4 3
♡ A K 10 7 6 ♡ Q 9 8 4
♢ 10 9 3 ♢ A 8 7 6 5 4
♣ 9 6 5 4 ♣ - - -

SOUTH
♠ A Q 9 8 5
♡ 5 3 2
♢ - - -
♣ A K J 3 2

West	North	East	South
			1♠
Pass	4♡ (1)	Pass	6♠
Pass	Pass	Pass	

(1) Splinter, 4+ spades, 0-1 heart

West leads the ♡A. East plays ♡4, asking for a club switch. If South plays the ♡5, West will need to deduce that the ♡4 is low. East is almost certain to have a higher heart available to signal for a diamond switch.

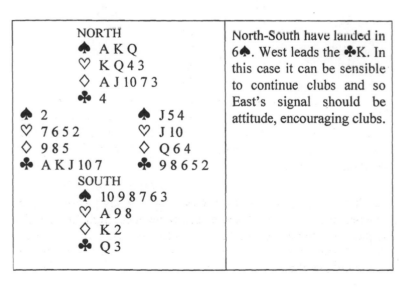

NORTH
♠ A K Q
♡ K Q 4 3
♢ A J 10 7 3
♣ 4

♠ 2   ♠ J 5 4
♡ 7 6 5 2 ♡ J 10
♢ 9 8 5 ♢ Q 6 4
♣ A K J 10 7 ♣ 9 8 6 5 2

SOUTH
♠ 10 9 8 7 6 3
♡ A 9 8
♢ K 2
♣ Q 3

North-South have landed in 6♠. West leads the ♣K. In this case it can be sensible to continue clubs and so East's signal should be attitude, encouraging clubs.

6. Suit-preference signals within the trump suit

In most cases the number of trumps held by the defenders is obvious or is immaterial. In such cases the defenders can use their trump cards as suit-preference signals. Here is a case in point:

Pairs event : Dealer South : Nil vulnerable

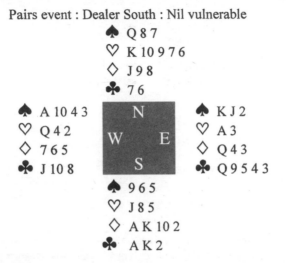

♠ Q 8 7
♡ K 10 9 7 6
♢ J 9 8
♣ 7 6

♠ A 10 4 3
♡ Q 4 2
♢ 7 6 5
♣ J 10 8

♠ K J 2
♡ A 3
♢ Q 4 3
♣ Q 9 5 4 3

♠ 9 6 5
♡ J 8 5
♢ A K 10 2
♣ A K 2

South opened 1NT, North bid 2♢, a transfer to hearts and South's 2♡ was passed out. West, Wladyslaw Izdebski, led the ♣J, taken by the ♣A. South played the ♡J: four – six – three, followed by the ♡8: two – seven – ace. Reading West's high-low in hearts as interest in the higher suit, spades, East switched to the ♠2, low-like. West won and returned a spade. The defence thus collected three spade tricks, which held South to nine tricks. At every other table declarer made ten tricks. If the defenders fail to attack spades early, South can discard one of dummy's spades on the fourth diamond.

The next deal arose in the final of a 2009 national team selection, where the defenders used a variety of signals successfully.

Dealer South : Both vulnerable

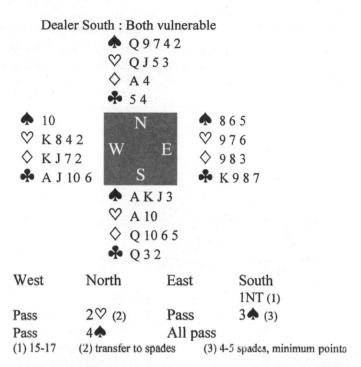

```
              ♠ Q 9 7 4 2
              ♡ Q J 5 3
              ◇ A 4
              ♣ 5 4
♠ 10                          ♠ 8 6 5
♡ K 8 4 2        N            ♡ 9 7 6
◇ K J 7 2    W     E          ◇ 9 8 3
♣ A J 10 6       S            ♣ K 9 8 7
              ♠ A K J 3
              ♡ A 10
              ◇ Q 10 6 5
              ♣ Q 3 2
```

West	North	East	South
			1NT (1)
Pass	2♡ (2)	Pass	3♠ (3)
Pass	4♠	All pass	

(1) 15-17   (2) transfer to spades   (3) 4-5 spades, minimum points

With no attractive lead, West began with the ♠10. South won and played the ♠3 to dummy's ♠9. West discarded the ◇2, suit-preference for clubs (playing even discards as suit-preference). Then came the ♡3 to the ♡10 and ♡K. How should West proceed?

West knew East could not have more than 3-4 points. On the spades East had played ♠5, then ♠6, the lowest card each time, suggesting interest in the lowest suit. West therefore shifted to the ♣6, low-like. East won and returned the ♣7. West captured South's ♣Q and the third club left South with a diamond loser for one down. At the other table West led the ◇2 against 4♠ and South made easily.

West: David Hoffman, East: Ron Klinger, both from Australia,

NORTH
♠ K Q 8 7 3
♡ 7 6 5
◇ A 3
♣ 8 7 6

♠ 9 5 2   ♠ A 4
♡ Q 4 3 2   ♡ J 10 9 8
◇ 10 9 2   ◇ 7 6 5 4
♣ A Q 9   ♣ J 10 4

SOUTH
♠ J 10 6
♡ A K
◇ K Q J 8
♣ K 5 3 2

Suit-preference within the trump suit can be extended to a trump opening lead.
South opened 1NT and reached 4♠ after a transfer sequence. West led the ♠2, deliberately the lowest to suggest values in the lowest suit, clubs. East won and switched to the ♣J and so declarer was down quickly.

NORTH
♠ K Q J
♡ K
◇ K 10 9 7 6 5 3
♣ Q 8

♠ 4   ♠ 10 8 5 3
♡ A J 10 6   ♡ 9 8 7 5 3 2
◇ 8 4   ◇ 2
♣ A 9 5 4 3 2   ♣ K 10

SOUTH
♠ A 9 7 6 2
♡ Q 4
◇ A Q J
♣ J 7 6

Even advanced players can have signalling difficulties. This example is from a Masters Tournament.

West	North	East	South
Pass	1◇	Pass	1♠
Dble	2◇	3♡	4◇
Pass	4♠	All pass	

West led the ♣A and the ♣10 from East was taken as high-discouraging. West switched to ♡A and another heart and so 4♠ made.
East said later, "I had no idea how to encourage you to continue clubs."
How could East solve it?

If we apply the rules suggested so far, then when dummy has a singleton, a suit-preference signal can apply. East should play the ♡2 under the ♡A at trick 2. If West recognises this as a request for clubs, West will revert to clubs. East wins and exits with the ◇2. East will now score a trump trick to defeat the contract.

What if West began with ♡A-8-6-3, South with ♡Q-9-4 and East's hand looked like this:

♠ A 9 5 3   ♡ J 10 7 5 2   ◇ 2   ♣ 10 7 3

Now East should play the ♡7 on the ♡A. We use the middle card from a known long suit as encouraging a continuation of that suit. If West continues hearts, South can win and lead a trump, but East wins and now a top heart, ruffed in dummy will create a trick for East later with the ♠9.

Our approach when signalling with a known long suit is high card = suit-preference, lowest card = suit-preference and a middle card asks partner to continue the suit. There are other approaches. Some use an odd card to ask for the suit to be continued and even cards in a known long suit are suit-preference. Using this method, East would play the ♡5 or ♡7 to ask West to continue hearts, the ♡10 would be suit preference for diamonds (perhaps East has a void) and the ♡2 would be suit-preference for clubs.

This method has a drawback that you might not always have a suitable odd or even card available. With a long suit, you will always have a middle card, but the question is, will partner always be able to pick that the card you play is a middling one.

Chapter 8
Suit-preference discards

Suit-preference discards, commonly known as Lavinthal discards or McKenney discards, are a popular method. A defender's discard indicates no interest in the suit discarded AND
(a) a high discard shows values in the higher-ranking suit, OR
(b) a low discard shows values in the lower-ranking suit.

This method is not always best:

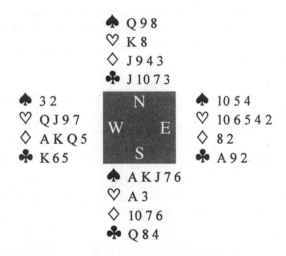

```
              ♠ Q 9 8
              ♡ K 8
              ◇ J 9 4 3
              ♣ J 10 7 3
  ♠ 3 2            N          ♠ 10 5 4
  ♡ Q J 9 7                   ♡ 10 6 5 4 2
  ◇ A K Q 5    W       E      ◇ 8 2
  ♣ K 6 5          S          ♣ A 9 2
              ♠ A K J 7 6
              ♡ A 3
              ◇ 10 7 6
              ♣ Q 8 4
```

South opened 1♠, double from West, 2♠ North, passed out. West began with ◇A, ◇K, ◇Q. What should East play on the ◇Q?

To discard the ♡2, suit-preference, will show strength in clubs, the lower-ranking suit outside trumps, but will not defeat 2♠.

Using suit-preference with your first discard is not very popular. Most defenders prefer to play high-low encouraging or reverse attitude within the suit discarded. Direct encouraging signals can work against suit contracts on some deals, but not all the time.

On the previous deal, playing high-encourage (discard the ♣9) or low-encourage (discard the ♣2) will create a club ruff and so defeat 2♠. A suit-preference discard will not help here.

However, if East had started with ♣A-9 doubleton, a discouraging signal in hearts suggests a club shift, but partner might simply continue with a fourth diamond. In this case a suit-preference ♡2 on the third diamond would definitely request a switch to clubs.

Likewise, if East had no values in clubs or hearts, but say, ♠K-J-x, a discouraging signal in hearts or clubs is likely to fetch a switch to the other suit. A suit-preference discard of a high heart or a low club will request partner to play the fourth diamond to eliminate dummy's winner in that suit.

Dealer South : East-West vulnerable

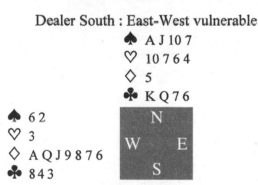

```
              ♠ A J 10 7
              ♡ 10 7 6 4
              ◇ 5
              ♣ K Q 7 6
  ♠ 6 2              N
  ♡ 3
  ◇ A Q J 9 8 7 6   W        E
  ♣ 8 4 3
                     S
```

South opens 1♠, West overcalls 3◇ and North's 4♣ is passed out. You, West lead the ♡3. Partner takes the ♡A, South playing ♡5, and returns the ♡2. You ruff South's ♡J. What next?

Obviously defenders must not treat discards mechanically or follow the suit-preference rules slavishly. In this case East's ♡2 is a suit-preference signal for clubs, but it does not guarantee that partner has the ♣A. Here is the complete deal:

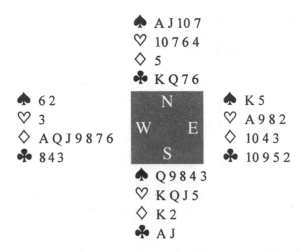

```
              ♠ A J 10 7
              ♡ 10 7 6 4
              ◇ 5
              ♣ K Q 7 6
♠ 6 2                            ♠ K 5
♡ 3              N               ♡ A 9 8 2
◇ A Q J 9 8 7 6   W      E       ◇ 10 4 3
♣ 8 4 3              S           ♣ 10 9 5 2
              ♠ Q 9 8 4 3
              ♡ K Q J 5
              ◇ K 2
              ♣ A J
```

After taking the ♡A, partner could not afford to return the ♡9 or ♡8 to give you a ruff. A high heart return would request a switch to the higher suit, diamonds, and would indicate the ◇K with East.

You should therefore cater for a layout, such as the one in the diagram above. After ruffing the heart return, cash the ◇A next and only then switch to a club. If partner does have the ♣A, your cashing the ◇A first will have done no harm to the defence.

While suit-preference discards work very well in no-trumps, you can often achieve the same result by using encourage/discourage discards as long as you apply a little commonsense. Consider the following deal:

Dealer South : Nil vulnerable

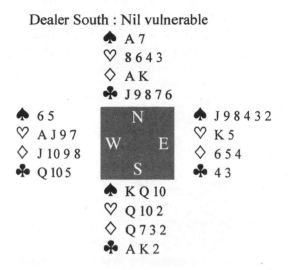

♠ A 7
♡ 8 6 4 3
♢ A K
♣ J 9 8 7 6

♠ 6 5
♡ A J 9 7
♢ J 10 9 8
♣ Q 10 5

♠ J 9 8 4 3 2
♡ K 5
♢ 6 5 4
♣ 4 3

♠ K Q 10
♡ Q 10 2
♢ Q 7 3 2
♣ A K 2

Against silent opposition, N-S bid 1NT : 2♣, 2♢ : 3NT, Pass. West leads the ♢J: king – six (high-discouraging) – three. Declarer plays ♣A, ♣K and a third club. West wins and East discards the ♠9 (high-discouraging). What should West do?

East has discouraged diamonds (♢6) and spades (♠9). Thus East implies interest in hearts. West shifts to the ♡7. East takes the ♡K and returns a heart to defeat 3NT. A suit-preference discard of the ♠9 (don't like spades, asks for the higher of the remaining suits) makes a switch to hearts even more emphatic.

A discard does not always carry an attitude or suit-preference meaning. A later chapter deals with interpretation of signals. Sometimes a defender will need to give count, especially when it concerns declarer's long suit, the main source of tricks.

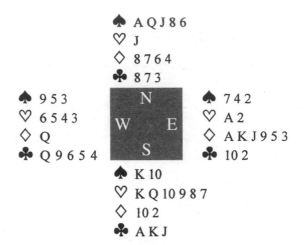

♠ A Q J 8 6
♡ J
◇ 8 7 6 4
♣ 8 7 3

♠ 9 5 3
♡ 6 5 4 3
◇ Q
♣ Q 9 6 5 4

♠ 7 4 2
♡ A 2
◇ A K J 9 5 3
♣ 10 2

♠ K 10
♡ K Q 10 9 8 7
◇ 10 2
♣ A K J

South opened 1♡, North responded 1♠ and East overcalled 2◇. South jumped to 3♡, North raised to 4♡ and all passed. West led the ◇Q, East overtook with the ◇K and continued with the ◇A. West discarded the ♠9, reverse count to show an odd number of spades. East now switched to a spade and, after taking the ♡A, played a second spade. This prevented declarer from taking a third trick in that suit. What if West and South had these cards:

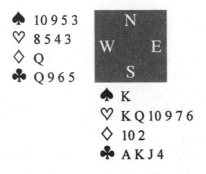

♠ 10 9 5 3
♡ 8 5 4 3
◇ Q
♣ Q 9 6 5

♠ K
♡ K Q 10 9 7 6
◇ 10 2
♣ A K J 4

Now West should ask partner to continue diamonds for a trump promotion of the ♡8 by discarding ♣9 to discourage a club switch.

Chapter 9
Trump control

In suit contracts the declaring side usually holds the majority of
trumps. It is not common for either defender to hold four trumps.
Four to the king or ace is considered a 'strong' position in defence
and is often enough to defeat declarer's powerful trump holding.

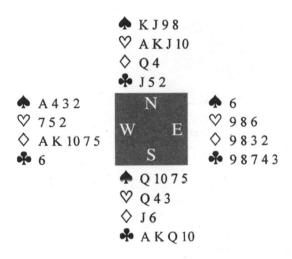

♠ K J 9 8
♡ A K J 10
◇ Q 4
♣ J 5 2

♠ A 4 3 2
♡ 7 5 2
◇ A K 10 7 5
♣ 6

♠ 6
♡ 9 8 6
◇ 9 8 3 2
♣ 9 8 7 4 3

♠ Q 10 7 5
♡ Q 4 3
◇ J 6
♣ A K Q 10

Contract: 4♠ by South. West began with ◇A, ◇K. What next? It
seems as though West has only one trump trick, but continuing
diamonds will produce a second trump trick for West, even
though the third diamond finds declarer with a void in each hand.

Declarer is obliged to ruff, let's say in dummy, and will start on
the trumps. West ducks the first two rounds of trumps. If South
plays a third trump, West now takes the ♠A. Dummy is out of
trumps, declarer has one. West plays another diamond. South can
ruff, but West scores the last trump and another diamond. Two off.

On seeing the bad trump split, South might abandon trumps after the second round and start on the heart and club winners. Now West ruffs the second club for one down. Note that South will succeed if West chooses the singleton club as the opening lead.

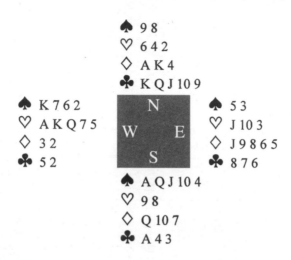

♠ 9 8
♡ 6 4 2
◇ A K 4
♣ K Q J 10 9

♠ K 7 6 2
♡ A K Q 7 5
◇ 3 2
♣ 5 2

♠ 5 3
♡ J 10 3
◇ J 9 8 6 5
♣ 8 7 6

♠ A Q J 10 4
♡ 9 8
◇ Q 10 7
♣ A 4 3

Contract: 4♠ by South after West had bid hearts. West starts with the ♡A, ♡K, ♡Q and South ruffs the third round. A diamond to dummy is followed by the ♠9, finessing. If West takes the ♠K and plays another heart, declarer will ruff in dummy, return to hand and, after drawing trumps, will take the remaining tricks.

West must duck the first round of trumps. Declarer will no doubt finesse again and now West pounces. South will have to trump the fourth heart in hand. West has thus gained trump control and will defeat 4♠ by two tricks.

It is easy to see the benefit of ducking with A-x-x-x or K-x-x-x in trumps. Sometimes you have to duck twice even with A-x-x:

```
           NORTH
        ♠ Q 10 9
        ♡ 7 3 2
        ◇ A K J 7
        ♣ J 5 4
WEST                EAST
♠ A 7 6             ♠ 5 4 3
♡ A K Q J           ♡ 9 8 5 4
◇ 5 3               ◇ 8 4
♣ 10 7 6 3          ♣ Q 9 8 2
           SOUTH
        ♠ K J 8 2
        ♡ 10 6
        ◇ Q 10 9 6 2
        ♣ A K
```

After South opened 1◇, West doubled, North redoubled and South ended in 4♠. West led ♡A, ♡K, ♡Q. South ruffed the third heart and played ♠K, ducked, followed by the ♠J. If West takes the ♠A now, 4♠ makes. No play by West poses any danger to South.

What if West ducks again? South cannot afford to play a third trump. That allows West to cash a heart winner. South will start on the diamonds and East ruffs the third round. The ♠A will be the fourth trick for the defence.

```
           NORTH
        ♠ 2
        ♡ K 10 7
        ◇ A K Q J 7
        ♣ 10 9 5 3
WEST                EAST
♠ A J 8 3           ♠ K Q 9 7 5
♡ Q 9 5             ♡ 8 6 2
◇ 9 8 6 2           ◇ 5 3
♣ 6 4               ♣ K 7 2
           SOUTH
        ♠ 10 6 4
        ♡ A J 4 3
        ◇ 10 4
        ♣ A Q J 8
```

In the hands of a skilled defender, Q-x-x in trumps might be enough to defeat declarer. Here is English star, Roman Smolski, in action. After North opened 1◇, East-West competed in spades and South ended in 4♡. West, Smolski, led the ♣6. South captured East's ♣K, crossed to the ♡K and led the ♡10, letting it run. Smolski played the ♡9 without hesitation!

When declarer repeated the heart finesse, the roof caved in. Smolski won the third round of hearts with the ♡Q and the defenders cashed three spade tricks for one down.

Here is a deal from the Rosenblum Cup semi-final between
Pakistan and the USA:

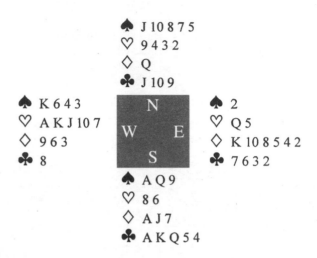

♠ J 10 8 7 5
♡ 9 4 3 2
◇ Q
♣ J 10 9

♠ K 6 4 3
♡ A K J 10 7
◇ 9 6 3
♣ 8

♠ 2
♡ Q 5
◇ K 10 8 5 4 2
♣ 7 6 3 2

♠ A Q 9
♡ 8 6
◇ A J 7
♣ A K Q 5 4

At one table everything went smoothly. West led the ♡A, ♡K
and ♡J against 4♠. South ruffed with the ♠Q and played the ♠9.
West ducked and declarer overtook with the ♠10. Dummy's
fourth heart was ruffed with the ♠A. A trick was lost later to the
♠K, but South had made the contract.

At the other table North was in 4♠ on a diamond lead. Fazli
(North for Pakistan) took the ◇A and, to retain trump control,
aimed to lose a trump trick early by leading the ♠Q. If West takes
the ♠K, the defence can take two heart tricks, but that is all.

Weichsel, West, ducked the ♠Q and ducked again when declarer
continued with the ♠9. Now North lost a spade and four hearts.

A similar situation arose on this deal from the Polish Trials. Cover the East-West cards and plan your play as South in 6♢. West leads the ♠Q. How do you handle the trump suit?

Suppose you start by playing the ♢5 to the ♢9, which wins the trick. How would you continue?

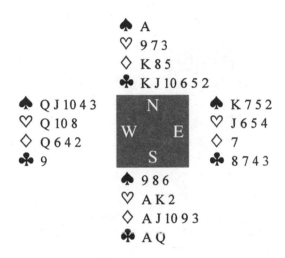

          ♠ A
          ♡ 9 7 3
          ♢ K 8 5
          ♣ K J 10 6 5 2

♠ Q J 10 4 3   ♠ K 7 5 2
♡ Q 10 8   ♡ J 6 5 4
♢ Q 6 4 2   ♢ 7
♣ 9   ♣ 8 7 4 3

          ♠ 9 8 6
          ♡ A K 2
          ♢ A J 10 9 3
          ♣ A Q

Andrzej Milde was South in 6♢. West, Krzysztof Lasocki, led the ♠Q, taken by the ♠A. Declarer played the ♢5 to the ♢9. Lasocki ducked smoothly. If South continues with a top trump, the slam will fail, but Milde took a safety play to ensure trump control. At trick 3 he returned the ♢3 to dummy's ♢8. Thus he made all thirteen tricks.

The next deal is from the final of the USA Selection Trials for the Bermuda Bowl:

Dealer South : Both vulnerable

♠ Q 6 2
♡ 10 9 8 7 4 2
♢ J 8 5
♣ 7

♠ K 10 8 7   ♠ A J 9 5 4 3
♡ Q J 3   N   ♡ A K 5
♢ 4 3   W   E   ♢ 10 9 2
♣ K Q 10 8   S   ♣ 2

♠ - - -
♡ 6
♢ A K Q 7 6
♣ A J 9 6 5 4 3

Table 1:

West	North	East	South
Wold	*Martell*	*Lair*	*Stansby*
			1♣
Pass	1♡	1♠	2♢
2♡ (1)	Pass	4♠	4NT
Pass	5♢	Pass	Pass
Double	Pass	Pass	Pass

(1)Good spade raise

Table 2:

West	North	East	South
Wolff	*Cohen*	*Hamman*	*Bergen*
			1♣
Pass	1♡	2♠	3♢
4♠	Pass	Pass	4NT
Pass	5♢	Double	All pass

At Table 1 Wold led a diamond to protect his club holding, but when declarer has a pronounced two-suiter with the shorter suit as trumps, it often pays to try to tap his trump holding. South won with the ◊J in dummy and tried to ruff two clubs. He went two down, losing two club over-ruffs, the ♡A and the ♣K.

South could have done better by winning the trump lead in hand and ruffing a club with the ◊J. Trumps are drawn and South loses one heart and two club tricks.

At Table 2 Wolff began with the theoretically better spade lead. He led the ♠7, low from dummy, and East played the ♠J. South ruffed, cashed the ♣A and ruffed a club with the ◊8. If East over-ruffs and shortens South with a spade, declarer can ruff a club with the ◊J, draw trumps and escape for one down.

East ducked the ◊8! South now played a heart from dummy. East won with the ♡K and returned a spade. South ruffed, ruffed a club with the ◊J, ruffed a heart to hand and ruffed another club.

This time Hamman over-ruffed and, down to the same number of trumps as South, he tapped him with another spade. The result was three off for East-West +800.

Fifteen years later, thanks to his partner, David Berkowitz, Larry Cohen was able to exact his revenge on Hamman. It took place on this deal from a Life Masters Pairs:

NORTH
♠ A
♡ J 6 3
♢ 10 6 4 3
♣ Q 9 8 4 3

WEST
♠ Q 9 8 2
♡ 7 4
♢ K Q J 7 2
♣ K 6

EAST
♠ 6 5
♡ K Q 10
♢ A 9 8
♣ J 10 7 5 2

SOUTH
♠ K J 10 7 4 3
♡ A 9 8 5 2
♢ 5
♣ A

South opened 1♠, North responded 1NT and South rebid 4♡, passed out. Cohen, West, began with the ♢K, followed by a low diamond.

Bob Hamman, South, ruffed, unblocked the ♠A, came to hand with the ♣A and played the ♠K. This was now the position (see next diagram):

NORTH
♠ ---
♡ J 6 3
♢ 10 6
♣ Q 9 8

WEST
♠ Q 9
♡ 7 4
♢ Q J 7
♣ K

EAST
♠ ---
♡ K Q 10
♢ 9
♣ J 10 7 5

SOUTH
♠ J 10 7 4
♡ A 9 8 5
♢ ---
♣ ---

South continued with the ♠J and, when West followed with the ♠9, declarer ruffed with dummy's ♡J. If Berkowitz over-ruffs, the defence will be finished. Declarer will ruff a minor suit return and ruff another spade in dummy.

A duck by East now is of no avail. Declarer has three trumps in hand and can claim.

Berkowitz ducked the ♡J and discarded a club. Declarer ruffed a club to hand and cashed the ♡A, leaving this ending (see next page):

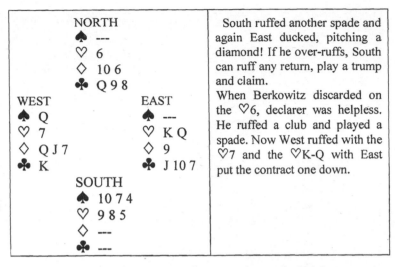

South ruffed another spade and again East ducked, pitching a diamond! If he over-ruffs, South can ruff any return, play a trump and claim.

When Berkowitz discarded on the ♡6, declarer was helpless. He ruffed a club and played a spade. Now West ruffed with the ♡7 and the ♡K-Q with East put the contract one down.

This deal illustrates how to exercise control over dummy's trumps:

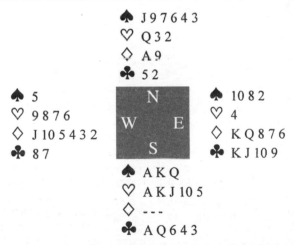

South was in 6♡ on the ♡9 lead. South took the ♡10 and the ♡A. When East showed out, South played ♠A, ♠K. West has to refuse to ruff, of course, and must again decline to ruff on the ♠Q to prevent South from enjoying dummy's long spades.

This deal comes from a Bermuda Bowl semi-final between France and Italy:

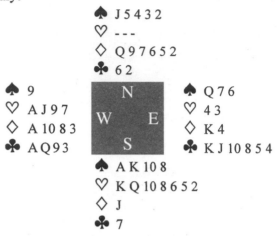

```
              ♠ J 5 4 3 2
              ♡ - - -
              ◇ Q 9 7 6 5 2
              ♣ 6 2
♠ 9                           ♠ Q 7 6
♡ A J 9 7          N          ♡ 4 3
◇ A 10 8 3      W     E       ◇ K 4
♣ A Q 9 3          S          ♣ K J 10 8 5 4
              ♠ A K 10 8
              ♡ K Q 10 8 6 5 2
              ◇ J
              ♣ 7
```

West	North	East	South
Soulet	*Franco*	*Lebel*	*De Falco*
		Pass	1♠ (1)
Double	4♠	5♣	5♡
Pass	5♠	Pass	Pass
Double	Pass	Pass	Pass

(1) Canape opening, shorter suit first

West led the ♣A, followed by the ♣3. South ruffed and played the ♡K, covered by the ♡A and ruffed in dummy. South returned to hand with a spade to the ace, cashed the ♡Q and ruffed the next heart with the ♠J. East discarded a club. A spade to the king was followed by another heart, ruffed in dummy. East discarded!

When declarer played a diamond from dummy, East rose with the ◇K and drew the remaining trumps with the ♠Q. The result was thus 800 to East-West!

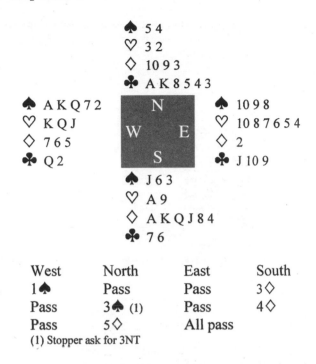

♠ 5 4
♡ 3 2
◇ 10 9 3
♣ A K 8 5 4 3

♠ A K Q 7 2   ♠ 10 9 8
♡ K Q J   ♡ 10 8 7 6 5 4
◇ 7 6 5   ◇ 2
♣ Q 2   ♣ J 10 9

♠ J 6 3
♡ A 9
◇ A K Q J 8 4
♣ 7 6

West	North	East	South
1♠	Pass	Pass	3◇
Pass	3♠ (1)	Pass	4◇
Pass	5◇	All pass	

(1) Stopper ask for 3NT

West starts off with the ♠A and ♣K. What next?

Many defenders will switch to the ♡K, after which declarer can succeed by setting up the club suit. After taking the ♡A, South cashes ◇A, ◇K, followed by the ♣A, ♣K and a third club, ruffed high. The ◇10 is the entry to enjoy dummy's club winners.

Those who remember the point about establishing control over dummy's trumps will play the ♠Q at trick 3. This forces declarer to ruff in dummy and now, with the diamonds 3-1, dummy's club length is dead.

To conclude this chapter, here is an example of fine declarer technique. Can we defeat South with skilful technique in defence?

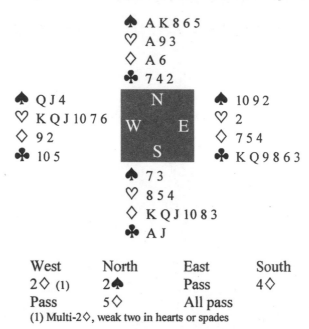

♠ A K 8 6 5
♡ A 9 3
◇ A 6
♣ 7 4 2

♠ Q J 4
♡ K Q J 10 7 6
◇ 9 2
♣ 10 5

♠ 10 9 2
♡ 2
◇ 7 5 4
♣ K Q 9 8 6 3

♠ 7 3
♡ 8 5 4
◇ K Q J 10 8 3
♣ A J

West	North	East	South
2◇ (1)	2♠	Pass	4◇
Pass	5◇	All pass	

(1) Multi-2◇, weak two in hearts or spades

South overbid, but compensated for that in the play. West led the ♡K and South ducked in dummy! The next heart was covered by the ♡A, ruffed by East, who switched to the ♣K.

The rest was easy. South took the ♣A, played off the ♠A and ♠K and ruffed the third spade. Now came the ◇K, followed by a diamond to the ace and the heart and club loser went away on dummy's spade winners.

South set a trap and East fell for it. You, the alert reader, have, of course, already spotted what mistake was made by East. He should not have ruffed the ♡A! That is a tough trap to avoid. East needed to ask himself why South had not taken the first heart.

Chapter 10
Trump tricks from nowhere

Try this problem:

♠ A K J 10
♡ 5 3
◇ A K 2
♣ A Q J 2

♠ Q 8 4 3
♡ J 2
◇ Q J 10 3
♣ 8 5 3

West	North	East	South
Pass	1♣ (1)	Pass	1◇ (2)
2♡	Double (3)	Pass	2♠
Pass	4♠	All pass	

(1) Artificial, strong   (2) Artificial, negative   (3) Takeout double

West leads the ♡Q, followed by the ♡A and the ♡K. Declarer ruffs the third heart with the ♠J. What would you do as East?

The instinctive move is to over-ruff with the ♠Q, but if you do, South will make the contract, because South began with:

♠ 7 6 5 2   ♡ 9 8 6   ◇ 7 5 4   ♣ K 9 4

You can see what will happen if you over-ruff with the ♠Q. South can draw trumps and make ten tricks. South is marked with the ♣K, else West would have opened the bidding. You have to hope West has the ♠9. If so, you will come to two trump tricks as long as you discard instead of over-ruffing the ♠J.

The previous deal is an example of a trump trick from nowhere when best defence allows your lowly ♠8 to score a trick. We can apply a general rule to this type of position: **With a top honour plus another high card such as the ten, nine or eight in trumps (and usually at least three or more trumps), do not over-ruff.**

Following this rule will often generate an extra trump trick.

Here are some more examples:

♠ 5 4 2

♠ K 9 3   ♠ 10 6

♠ A Q J 8 7

If South ruffs with the jack or queen, it costs West a trick to over-ruff. By discarding West can score two trump tricks.

This is a tougher position in practice:

♠ Q J 4

♠ 10 5   ♠ K 9 3

♠ A 8 7 6 2

If dummy ruffs with the ♠Q and East over-ruffs, that it is the only trump trick for East-West. If East declines to over-ruff, the defence scores two trump tricks. The problem for East is that the location of the ♠10 is not known.

♠ J 5 4

♠ Q   ♠ K 10 7 3

♠ A 9 8 6 2

If dummy ruffs with the ♠J and East over-ruffs, the defence takes two trump tricks only. If East does not over-ruff, the defence can come to three trump tricks.

NORTH
♠ K 10 9
♡ J 3
♢ A K 7 6 5
♣ K 3 2

WEST
♠ - - -
♡ A K Q 10 6 5
♢ 10 9 4 2
♣ 9 5 4

EAST
♠ Q J 7 5
♡ 8 4
♢ 8 3
♣ Q J 8 7 6

SOUTH
♠ A 8 6 4 3 2
♡ 9 7 2
♢ Q J
♣ A 10

South ended up in 4♠. West started with the three top hearts and declarer ruffed the third round with the ♠10. If you over-ruff with the ♠J, declarer will later finesse against your ♠Q and make 4♠. If you discard a diamond instead, 4♠ will be defeated.

NORTH
♠ 7 4 3
♡ J 3 2
♢ A K 9 4
♣ 9 5 2

WEST
♠ - - -
♡ 9 5 4
♢ 10 7 5 3 2
♣ A K 10 8 6

EAST
♠ K 10 9 6
♡ Q 10 8 7 6
♢ Q 8
♣ 7 3

SOUTH
♠ A Q J 8 5 2
♡ A K
♢ J 6
♣ Q J 4

Sometimes not over-ruffing creates an extra trick by complicating declarer's life. See what happened on this deal to Terence Reese in a European Open Teams: Both tables led ♣A, ♣K and a third club ruffed by East. Declarer later finessed twice against East to make the contract. Reese later worked out that if he had discarded a diamond instead of ruffing, he would have come to two trump tricks, as declarer would now have only one entry to dummy.

NORTH
♠ Q
♡ A J 10 5
◇ K J 10 9 4 2
♣ K Q

WEST
♠ J 10 9 8 5 4 2
♡ 3
◇ A 8
♣ A 9 8

EAST
♠ 3
♡ K 9 7 6
◇ Q 6 5 3
♣ 10 4 3 2

SOUTH
♠ A K 7 6
♡ Q 8 4 2
◇ 7
♣ J 7 6 5

One of the co-authors of this book failed to follow the general rule (page 126) to his detriment in the 1988 Zakopane Congress. North opened 1◇, South bid 1♡, 3♠ by West and 4♡ North, all pass. Dummy won the ♠J lead and South played the ♣K. West took the ♣A and played the ♠10, ruffed in dummy and over-ruffed by East, 4♡ now made. If East discards a club instead of over-ruffing, 4♡ can be defeated.

NORTH
♠ K 2
♡ Q 4
◇ A K Q 7 6
♣ K 8 4 2

WEST
♠ 8
♡ A K J 10 8 7 6
◇ 10 2
♣ J 9 6

EAST
♠ Q 9 7 5 4 3
♡ 5 3
◇ 9 8 5 3
♣ 10

SOUTH
♠ A J 10 6
♡ 9 2
◇ J 4
♣ A Q 7 5 3

Another way to create an extra trump trick is via an 'uppercut': a defender with short trumps ruffs high and forces declarer to over-ruff.

West	North	East	South
			1♣
3♡	4◇	Pass	4♠
Pass	5♣	All pass	

West starts with ♡A, ♡K. What next? South is sure to have the black aces. If East has the ♣Q, we have a sure trick, but actually the ♣10 will do. Play a third heart. East ruffs with the ♣10 and West has a trump trick.

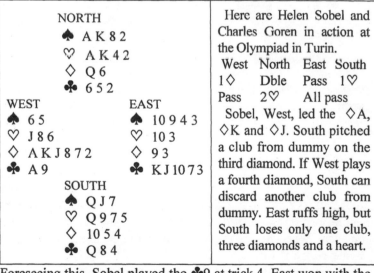

NORTH
♠ 8 6 3 2
♡ A Q J
♢ K 5 4
♣ 7 6 4

WEST
♠ A K Q 9 7
♡ 8 7
♢ Q J 9 3
♣ J 2

EAST
♠ J 10
♡ 10 9 6 5 3
♢ 10 8 7 6
♣ Q 3

SOUTH
♠ 5 4
♡ K 4 2
♢ A 2
♣ A K 10 9 8 5

West	North	East	South
1♠	Pass	Pass	3♣
Pass	3♠	Pass	4♣
Pass	5♣	All pass	

West starts with the ♠A, ♠K. How should West continue to try to beat 5♣? By an uppercut promotion. West needs East to hold the ♣Q or ♣K. To force East to ruff, West plays a low spade next. This asks East to ruff high. After East ruffs with the ♣Q, the defence has a trump trick.

NORTH
♠ A K 8 2
♡ A K 4 2
♢ Q 6
♣ 6 5 2

WEST
♠ 6 5
♡ J 8 6
♢ A K J 8 7 2
♣ A 9

EAST
♠ 10 9 4 3
♡ 10 3
♢ 9 3
♣ K J 10 7 3

SOUTH
♠ Q J 7
♡ Q 9 7 5
♢ 10 5 4
♣ Q 8 4

Here are Helen Sobel and Charles Goren in action at the Olympiad in Turin.

West	North	East	South
1♢	Dble	Pass	1♡
Pass	2♡	All pass	

Sobel, West, led the ♢A, ♢K and ♢J. South pitched a club from dummy on the third diamond. If West plays a fourth diamond, South can discard another club from dummy. East ruffs high, but South loses only one club, three diamonds and a heart.

Foreseeing this, Sobel played the ♣9 at trick 4. East won with the ♣K and returned a club. Now another diamond defeated 2♡.

Here is a more difficult deal:

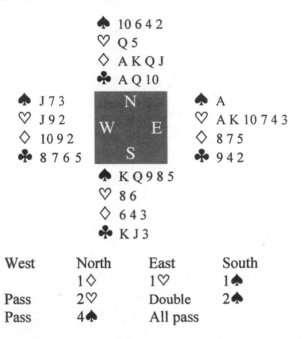

West	North	East	South
	1◇	1♡	1♠
Pass	2♡	Double	2♠
Pass	4♠	All pass	

West leads a heart, the ♡2 to deny a doubleton or, if you play reverse count leads, the ♡9. East wins with the ♡K and cashes the ♡A. It is now clear to East that West began with three hearts and hence both dummy and declarer are void in hearts. How should East continue?

East can see that the defence has no tricks coming in diamonds or clubs and so a switch to either of those suits is futile. There is no benefit in playing the ♠A. If West has a spade trick, it will not run away. When all else is clearly futile, pursue the long suit. East should play a third heart. Declarer can ruff in dummy and lead a spade, but when East takes the ♠A a fourth heart will create a trump trick for West to defeat the contract.

Here is a very deep promotion from a world championship match between Italy and the USA:

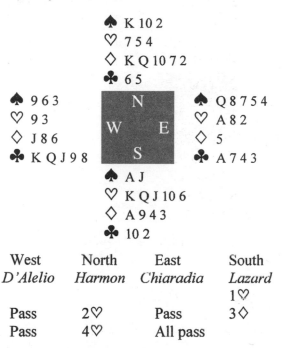

♠ K 10 2
♡ 7 5 4
◇ K Q 10 7 2
♣ 6 5

♠ 9 6 3
♡ 9 3
◇ J 8 6
♣ K Q J 9 8

♠ Q 8 7 5 4
♡ A 8 2
◇ 5
♣ A 7 4 3

♠ A J
♡ K Q J 10 6
◇ A 9 4 3
♣ 10 2

West	North	East	South
D'Alelio	Harmon	Chiaradia	Lazard
			1♡
Pass	2♡	Pass	3◇
Pass	4♡	All pass	

West led the ♣K and East overtook with the ace to shift to the singleton diamond. He planned to win the ♡A, cross to partner in clubs and receive a diamond ruff. South saw through this plan and played ♠A, ♠K and ♠10. When East played the ♠Q, South discarded his remaining club, a brilliant scissors coup to cut the communication between East and West.

Chiaradia was not done with yet. He worked out that he could still defeat 4♡ if partner had ♡9-x. East played a fourth spade. South ruffed with the ♡K and played the ♡Q. East won and persisted with another spade. South had to ruff high and so the ♡8 became the setting trick.

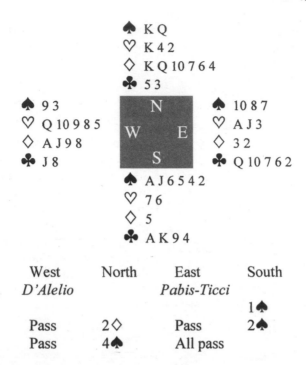

```
              ♠ K Q
              ♡ K 4 2
              ◇ K Q 10 7 6 4
              ♣ 5 3
♠ 9 3              N              ♠ 10 8 7
♡ Q 10 9 8 5                     ♡ A J 3
◇ A J 9 8      W       E         ◇ 3 2
♣ J 8              S              ♣ Q 10 7 6 2
              ♠ A J 6 5 4 2
              ♡ 7 6
              ◇ 5
              ♣ A K 9 4
```

West	North	East	South
D'Alelio		*Pabis-Ticci*	
			1♠
Pass	2◇	Pass	2♠
Pass	4♠	All pass	

West led the ♡9 (underleading): two – three – six. West continued with a heart and South ruffed the third heart. He played a low diamond and West took the ace. When the fourth heart came, South ruffed in dummy and discarded a club, while East threw his last diamond.

Dummy's ◇K came next. East ruffed and South over-ruffed. A spade to dummy was followed by the ◇Q. East ruffed again and thus West's ♠9 was promoted to the fourth trick for the defence.

Suppose South ruffs the fourth round of hearts in hand, as East discards the second diamond. Declarer cannot ruff two clubs in dummy or try to discard them on dummy's diamond without incurring a trump promotion of West's ♠9.

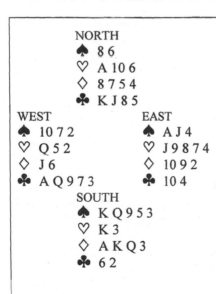

```
              NORTH
              ♠ 8 7
              ♡ 9 5
              ◇ J 10 6 5 4 2
              ♣ A K 6
WEST                        EAST
♠ A 9 6                     ♠ J 3
♡ A K 8 7 4                 ♡ J 6 2
◇ 8 3                       ◇ 9 7
♣ J 4 2                     ♣ Q 10 9 7 5 3
              SOUTH
              ♠ K Q 10 5 4 2
              ♡ Q 10 3
              ◇ A K Q
              ♣ 8
```

Now take a look at a fine defence by Michael Perron:

West	North	East	South
			1♠
Pass	1NT	Pass	3♠
Pass	4♠	All pass	

Perron, West, started with three rounds of hearts. South ruffed the third round in dummy and played a spade to the ten and ace. When Perron played the fourth heart, East ruffed with the ♠J and now the ♠9 set the contract.

```
              NORTH
              ♠ 8 6
              ♡ A 10 6
              ◇ 8 7 5 4
              ♣ K J 8 5
WEST                        EAST
♠ 10 7 2                    ♠ A J 4
♡ Q 5 2                     ♡ J 9 8 7 4
◇ J 6                       ◇ 10 9 2
♣ A Q 9 7 3                 ♣ 10 4
              SOUTH
              ♠ K Q 9 5 3
              ♡ K 3
              ◇ A K Q 3
              ♣ 6 2
```

Next, an Italian genius:
After bidding spades and diamonds, N-S have ended in 4♠. This is a poor spot, but trumps are 3-3, the ♠A is onside, so is the ♣A-Q and the diamonds are 3-2. The only bad feature was Giorgio Belladonna sat East. The ♡2 went to the king and a club to the jack held. A spade to the king was followed by a heart to the ace and another spade. East took the ♠A, led a club to the ace and ruffed the next club with the ♠J. One off.

```
                NORTH
             ♠ 4
             ♡ 10 8 3
             ◇ K J 9
             ♣ A K Q 9 6 5
WEST                        EAST
♠ K 10 2                    ♠ 9 3
♡ A K Q 9 6 4               ♡ 7 2
◇ 8 3                       ◇ 7 6 5 4 2
♣ 4 3                       ♣ J 10 8 7
                SOUTH
             ♠ A Q J 8 7 6 5
             ♡ J 5
             ◇ A Q 10
             ♣ 2
```

West	North	East	South
			1♠
2♡	3♣	Pass	4♠
Pass	Pass	Pass	

You start with the ♡A, ♡K. What next?

Play a third heart. If East has the ♠9 and ruffs with it, South over-ruffs and West's ♠K-10-x will yield two tricks.

West would play the same way with ♠K-9-2 and hope East could ruff with the ♠10 or ♠J and uppercut South.

```
                NORTH
             ♠ Q J 10 7
             ♡ K Q 10 9
             ◇ Q J
             ♣ 9 5 4
WEST                        EAST
♠ 8 4                       ♠ K 9 5
♡ 8 6 3 2                   ♡ 7 5
◇ 7 6 5 4 2                 ◇ 10 9 8
♣ 10 6                      ♣ A K Q 8 7
                SOUTH
             ♠ A 6 3 2
             ♡ A J 4
             ◇ A K 3
             ♣ J 3 2
```

The same opportunities exist for East.

West	North	East	South
			1NT*
Pass	2♣	Dble	2♠
Pass	4♠	All pass	

*15-17

West leads the ♣10 and East takes three club tricks. As West cannot hold more than the ♡J with the points on display and with South, East plays a fourth club. If holding the ♠8, West can ruff and uppercut dummy to produce a trump trick for East.

	NORTH	
	♠ K J 10 6	
	♥ K Q J 5	
	◇ K 4	
	♣ 9 8 4	
WEST		EAST
♠ 8 3		♠ Q 9 4
♥ 9 8 4		♥ 10 6 3
◇ 10 9 8 7 5		◇ J 3 2
♣ 5 3 2		♣ A K Q J
	SOUTH	
	♠ A 7 5 2	
	♥ A 7 2	
	◇ A Q 6	
	♣ 10 7 6	

The same defence is just as successful on this deal. South opened the bidding and is in 4♠. West leads a club and East collects three club tricks.

As it is clear to East that West cannot hold an ace, East continues with the fourth club. West ruffs with the ♠8 and creates a trump trick for East.

	NORTH	
	♠ 7 5 3	
	♥ 10 9 6	
	◇ K J 8 3	
	♣ A J 4	
WEST		EAST
♠ K 8 4		♠ 9 6
♥ 8 4		♥ A K Q J 5 2
◇ 10 9 7 6 2		◇ A 5
♣ 7 6 2		♣ 9 8 3
	SOUTH	
	♠ A Q J 10 2	
	♥ 7 3	
	◇ Q 4	
	♣ K Q 10 5	

Here is a refusal to over-ruff and a trump promotion on the same deal. South opens 1♠ and ends in 3♠ after East has bid hearts.

West leads the ♥8 and East plays three rounds of hearts. South ruffs the third with the ♠Q. If West over-ruffs, East scores the ◇A, but that is all and 3♠ makes. West should discard a club instead. South crosses to dummy in clubs and takes the spade finesse. West wins, plays a diamond to East and the next heart promotes a trump for West.

Sometimes there are opportunities for a trump promotion or an uppercut, but you cannot tell whether it will be successful or not. If all else appears to be futile, by all means continue with your long suit. Even though there is no certainty of success, you might give declarer a losing option.

Consider declarer's problem with this trump suit when West leads a suit in which dummy, East and declarer are void:

♠ 10 7 6

♠ A K Q 4

Should declarer ruff with dummy's ten or discard from dummy and ruff in hand? If declarer ruffs with the ten, the situation could be like this:

♠ 10 7 6

♠ 8 5 3   ♠ J 9 2

♠ A K Q 4

East covers the ten, South captures the jack and West scores a trick with the eight. The winning play here is not to ruff in dummy, but failing to ruff in dummy loses if the East-West holdings are reversed:

♠ 10 7 6

♠ J 8 3   ♠ 9 5 2

♠ A K Q 4

South needs to ruff with dummy's ten. If South discards from dummy, East ruffs with the nine and uppercuts South to create a trick for West's jack. South has the same problem in this layout:

West leads a suit where all the others are void. Declarer needs to ruff with the ten to escape an uppercut, but ruffing with the ten loses a trick when the layout is like this:

If South ruffs with the ten, East over-ruffs and South wins. Now West's nine has been promoted.

Declarer faces the same dilemma here:

♠ J 3 2

♠ A K 9 8 7 5

Ruffing with the jack loses to queen bare or queen doubleton with East, but not ruffing in dummy loses to Q-x with West and 10-x with East. You can see how continuing a long suit can give you a chance to create a trump trick from nowhere.

Sometimes declarer has no winning option. Look at this layout:

If declarer ruffs with the jack, East will score the ten later. If declarer does not ruff with the jack, East plays the ten and West's queen has become promoted.

Finally here is a deal where there is no trump promotion. But the defence still collects an extra trump trick from nowhere:

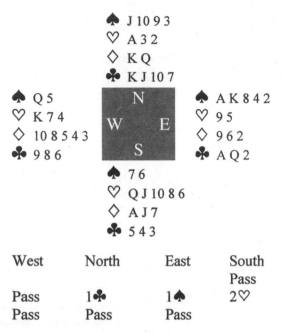

♠ J 10 9 3
♡ A 3 2
◇ K Q
♣ K J 10 7

♠ Q 5
♡ K 7 4
◇ 10 8 5 4 3
♣ 9 8 6

♠ A K 8 4 2
♡ 9 5
◇ 9 6 2
♣ A Q 2

♠ 7 6
♡ Q J 10 8 6
◇ A J 7
♣ 5 4 3

West	North	East	South
			Pass
Pass	1♣	1♠	2♡
Pass	Pass	Pass	

West leads the ♠Q, which wins, and continues with the ♠5, taken by the king. East returns the lowest spade and, with no useful discard, South ruffs with the ♡Q. Can you see any way to defeat the contract?

If West over-ruffs, the defence takes two spades, two clubs and a heart, five tricks only. East's low spade at trick 3 suggests suit-preference for clubs, probably with the ♣A-Q. What if West discards a club instead of over-ruffing? As long as West's play has been smooth, South is likely to place the ♡K with East. If South continues with a heart to the ace, followed by a low heart, West wins with the king, shifts to a club and scores a club ruff. One down!

Chapter 11
Quality vs Quantity

In the middle game, if you consider that the quality of the suit you
are about to lead is more important than the number of cards held,
it is standard to lead your lowest card to show interest in the suit
led. For example:

	NORTH				West	North	East	South
	♠ 10 8 4 3							1◇ (1)
	♡ Q 7				Pass	1♠	Pass	1NT
	◇ 7 2				Pass	2NT	Pass	3NT
	♣ A K J 10 5				Pass	Pass	Pass	

WEST leads the ♡5 and the ♡Q wins. South plays the ◇2 to the queen and king. What should West do?

```
              NORTH
              ♠ 10 8 4 3
              ♡ Q 7
              ◇ 7 2
              ♣ A K J 10 5
WEST                        EAST
♠ K 7 6                     ♠ A Q 9 2
♡ K J 6 5 4                 ♡ 10 3 2
◇ K 8 4 3                   ◇ 6 5
♣ 8                         ♣ 7 4 3 2
              SOUTH
              ♠ J 5
              ♡ A 9 8
              ◇ A Q J 10 9
              ♣ Q 9 6
```

West North East South
                         1◇ (1)
Pass 1♠   Pass 1NT
Pass 2NT   Pass 3NT
Pass Pass   Pass
(1) 5+ diamonds

West leads the ♡5 and the ♡Q wins. South plays the ◇2 to the queen and king. What should West do?

Looking at all four hands, it is obvious that a spade switch is needed, but most players will continue with a heart in the hope that East has the ♣Q.

West can tell that South has the ◇A, else East would have played
it in order to return a heart. As 1◇ showed 5+ diamonds, South is
known to have four diamond tricks, two clubs and two hearts. If
South has the ♠A, there is no hope, so assume East has the ♠A.

West should switch to the ♠6, lowest to show interest in spades.
East wins and returns the ♠2. The defence takes four spade tricks
and 3NT is one down.

Leading from the king will not do any damage if South holds:

♠ Q J 5   ♡ A 9 8   ♢ A Q J 10 9   ♣ 9 6

If partner has the ♣Q, but poor spades, East will take the ♠A and revert to hearts.

What if the full deal looked like this:

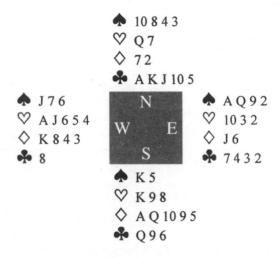

After the same auction and play to the first two tricks (♡5 lead, taken by the ♡Q, diamond to the queen and king) West figures that a heart return from East is needed to defeat 3NT. How can West pass this information to East? The clearest way is by leading the ♠J! With the ♠10 in dummy, the ♠J cannot be from a sequence and so the ♠J switch informs East that West has no desire to have spades continued. East should therefore take the ♠A and return a heart as the only chance to beat the contract.

Here are some examples where attitude is more important than count when broaching a new suit:

♣ K 10

♣ Q 7 5   ♣ A J 6 4 2

♣ 9 8 3

West leads the five, lowest to promise an honour. If the ten is played from dummy, East plays the jack. To lead the queen is an error. Declarer covers with the king and comes to a trick in the suit.

Leading low is also correct here:

♣ K 8

♣ Q 7 5   ♣ A 9 6 4 2

♣ J 10 3

West leads the five, low from dummy, ace. East returns the suit and declarer is held to one trick. If West leads the queen initially, it is covered by the king and South makes two tricks.

♢ 6 5 4

♢ A J 9 2   ♢ Q 7 3

♢ K 10 8

When East leads the ♢3, West knows to continue the suit if South plays the king.

♢ 6 5 4

♢ A J 9 2   ♢ 8 7 3

♢ K Q 10

In this layout, East should lead the ♢8, high-hate. When South plays the king, West should play the ♢2, low-like, to ask partner to continue the suit when on lead again later.

To sum up:

In the middle game in no-trumps or against a suit contract when it is obvious there is no hope for a ruff, low-encouraging, high-discouraging signals are used when leading a new suit.

Let's take a look at a situation where count signals take priority:

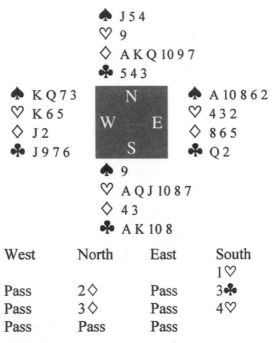

♠ J 5 4			
♡ 9			
◇ A K Q 10 9 7			
♣ 5 4 3			

West	North	East	South
			1♡
Pass	2◇	Pass	3♣
Pass	3◇	Pass	4♡
Pass	Pass	Pass	

West leads the ♠K.

When declarer is known to hold two suits, at least 5-4, count signals should be played when the lead is in an unbid suit.

East should play the ♠8 to show an odd number of spades. Knowing South has at least a 6-4 pattern in hearts-clubs, West will switch to a diamond at trick 2. When in with the ♡K, West will play another diamond to prevent South using dummy's diamond length. Now South cannot escape two losers in clubs.

The previous rule does not apply when:

(1) The second suit is a trial bid and need not be a genuine suit. For example:

West	North	East	South
			1♠
1NT	2♠	Pass	3♦...

South's 3♦ is a game invitation, usually based on just a 3-card suit, headed by one top honour or perhaps no honour at all. It could even be a psyche (a bluff bid).

(2) Partner showed a 5+ suit and you retain the lead. For example:

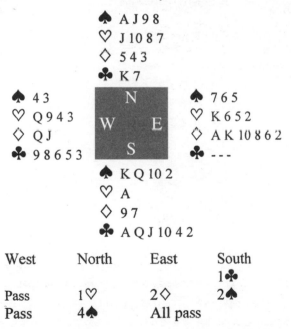

```
                ♠ A J 9 8
                ♡ J 10 8 7
                ◇ 5 4 3
                ♣ K 7
♠ 4 3          N          ♠ 7 6 5
♡ Q 9 4 3   W     E      ♡ K 6 5 2
◇ Q J                    ◇ A K 10 8 6 2
♣ 9 8 6 5 3    S          ♣ - - -
                ♠ K Q 10 2
                ♡ A
                ◇ 9 7
                ♣ A Q J 10 4 2
```

West	North	East	South
			1♣
Pass	1♡	2◇	2♠
Pass	4♠	All pass	

West leads the ◇Q. If using the recommendations in Chapter 9 (Suit-Preference Signals), East encourages diamonds by playing a middle card, while a high card or the lowest is suit-preference.

In this case East should play the ♦2 at trick 1 to ask for a club switch. West switches to the ♣3, lowest to ask for a diamond return. East ruffs, plays a low diamond to West and receives another club ruff.

Where two signalling systems are available, it makes sense to apply the one with a better chance of success.

At the five-level or higher, it is superior to play count. Declarer usually has a long suit to run and to keep the right cards, you need to know declarer's shape. The defenders often know all about the location of missing honours or the need to adopt a passive game. In these situations, count signals work best.

Here is an example from match-pointed pairs:

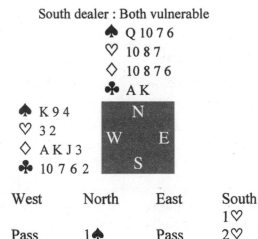

South dealer : Both vulnerable

```
                    ♠ Q 10 7 6
                    ♡ 10 8 7
                    ♦ 10 8 7 6
                    ♣ A K
        ♠ K 9 4          N
        ♡ 3 2
        ♦ A K J 3   W         E
        ♣ 10 7 6 2       S
```

West	North	East	South
			1♡
Pass	1♠	Pass	2♡
Pass	4♡	All pass	

You lead the ♦A: six – five – two. You continue with the ♦K: seven – four – nine. Partner has played ♦5-♦4. What next?

East has shown three diamonds. With a 4-card suit in dummy, it is best to signal count. With a doubleton, South would have played ♢4-♢5, encouraging, for a ruff, and count simultaneously.

There are two chances to defeat the contract:

(1) Partner has a heart trick and you will come to a spade trick if declarer has this hand for example:

♠ A J 5   ♡ K Q J 9 6 5   ♢ 9 2   ♣ Q J 4

(2) Suppose declarer holds:

♠ A 5 3   ♡ A Q J 9 6 5   ♢ 9 2   ♣ J 4

Assuming West ducks smoothly when declarer leads a low spade and declarer plays the ♠10 from dummy, the defence will come to two spade tricks.

The trouble is that by playing low on the first round of spades, you might concede an overtrick if South has:

♠ A 5   ♡ A Q 9 6 5 4   ♢ 9 2   ♣ Q 8 4

When declarer starts on the spades, if West plays low, South will always rise with dummy's ♠Q.

It follows that you should not play a third round of diamonds. South will ruff and if South now plays a low spade, you have no idea whether to play low or grab the king.

Playing teams the overtrick is of little consequence and you can shift to a heart to see whether East has a trick there. If not, you duck regardless when South plays a low spade.

At pairs, the best play is a club at trick 3. Partner should give you count on this and that will enables you to judge declarer's hand pattern. If partner shows an odd number of clubs, you deduce that South began with a 3-6-2-2 pattern and you will then duck when South plays a low spade.

If partner plays a low club, showing an even number of clubs, you place South with a 2-6-2-3 pattern and you thus know to rise with the ♠K when declarer leads low.

This is the complete deal:

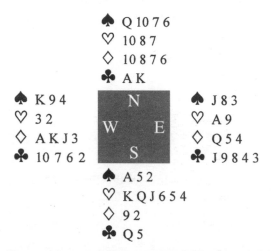

At trick 3 West switched to the ♣2 (also count, to help partner work out the hand shapes, too). East played the ♣9, a clear count signal, indicating an odd number of clubs. Declarer played a heart from dummy and East rose with the ♡A at once, to prevent any possibility of an endplay later. East returned the ♣3.

South came to hand with a heart and led the ♠2. West was ready for this and followed with the ♠9 smoothly. Declarer played the ♠10 from dummy. East won and returned a spade for two down, a top board.

Attitude or count? We cannot answer this question with 100% certainty. It will depend on the actual deal. It is up to each of the defenders to judge which information is more valuable for partner.

Chapter 12
Unusual play by third hand

We learned the 'third hand high' rule when we were beginners, but as usual there are exceptions.

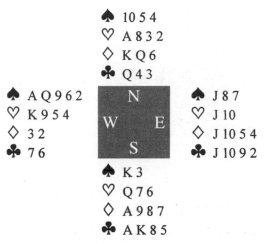

♠ 10 5 4
♥ A 8 3 2
♦ K Q 6
♣ Q 4 3

♠ A Q 9 6 2   ♠ J 8 7
♥ K 9 5 4   ♥ J 10
♦ 3 2   ♦ J 10 5 4
♣ 7 6   ♣ J 10 9 2

♠ K 3
♥ Q 7 6
♦ A 9 8 7
♣ A K 8 5

South opened 1NT, North raised to 3NT and West leads the ♠6. Declarer plays low from dummy and East's almost automatic play is the jack. South wins and plays off the top three cards in each minor. When neither splits 3-3, South exits with a spade. West can take four spade tricks, but is then end-played in hearts.

It was so easy to avoid this calamity by preserving the ♠J as East. How could East tell at trick 1? When we lead fourth-highest, simply applying the Rule of 11 will supply the answer. Declarer can have only one card higher than the six.

Can it be the ♠9? Of course not, else partner's spades would be headed by the A-K-Q and West would not lead low from that holding. Therefore, playing the jack at trick 1 could gain nothing.

	NORTH	
	♠ A Q	
	♡ Q 7 4 3 2	
	◇ J 9 2	
	♣ J 8 4	
WEST		EAST
♠ 9 8 7		♠ K 6 5 3 2
♡ K 10 9 6		♡ 8 5
◇ A 10 4		◇ 8 7 6 3
♣ K 9 2		♣ 6 5
	SOUTH	
	♠ J 10 4	
	♡ A J	
	◇ K Q 5	
	♣ A Q 10 7 3	

South is in 3NT again and West leads the ♠9: queen – king . . . and this is the end of the defence. East's spades can be set up, but East has no entry to cash the winners. The right move is to for East to duck the ♠Q and play an encouraging signal. West will continue spades twice as West gains the lead and the defence will collect three spades and West's two tricks.

	NORTH	
	♠ A 9 3	
	♡ Q J 10 9	
	◇ A 10 6	
	♣ Q J 5	
WEST		EAST
♠ 8 4		♠ K 10 7 6 2
♡ K 8 6 4		♡ A 7
◇ J 7 5 2		◇ Q 8 4
♣ 9 6 3		♣ 10 8 7
	SOUTH	
	♠ Q J 5	
	♡ 5 3 2	
	◇ K 9 3	
	♣ A K 4 2	

Here is the same situation in another guise. South is in 3NT once more and West leads the ♠8: low from dummy . . . If East wins with the king and returns a spade, West's lead will be wasted. Declarer will play hearts next. If West wins, there is no spade left. If East wins, the spades can be set up, but there is no entry to enjoy them. East should duck the first spade, but signal encouragement.

West wins the first heart and continues the spades. Now the defence can establish three spade tricks and East's ♡A is the entry.

NORTH
♠ A J 9
♡ 6 4 3
◇ J 10 9 7 2
♣ A K

WEST
♠ 7 5 4 3
♡ 8 2
◇ K 4
♣ 9 6 5 3 2

EAST
♠ Q 6 2
♡ K Q 10 9 7
◇ A 5
♣ J 7 4

SOUTH
♠ K 10 8
♡ A J 5
◇ Q 8 6 3
♣ Q 10 8

West	North	East	South
	1◇	1♡	3NT
Pass	Pass	Pass	

West leads the ♡8. If East plays the 'automatic' ♡Q, South ducks. If East plays a low heart next, South finesses the ♡J and 3NT cannot be beaten. This is like the previous deal and the mistake came at trick 1. East should play the ♡9. South takes the ♡J and plays a diamond. West wins and returns a heart. Now East's hearts will set up with the ◇A as entry.

NORTH
♠ Q 5 3 2
♡ 9 8 5
◇ A 5
♣ K Q J 10

WEST
♠ K J 8 4
♡ A 7 3
◇ 9 6 4 2
♣ 9 5

EAST
♠ 10 9 7 6
♡ 6
◇ K 10 8 7 3
♣ A 8 4

SOUTH
♠ A
♡ K Q J 10 4 2
◇ Q J
♣ 7 6 3 2

West	North	East	South
			1♡
Pass	1♠	Pass	2♡
Pass	4♡	All pass	

West leads the ♣9. If East takes the ace at trick 1, the contract will succeed. West's ♣9 is more likely to top from a doubleton than a singleton. West needs a quick trump entry and a quick entry to East for the ruff. East's only quick entry is the ♣A. East needs to preserve it by playing low and encouraging at trick 1.

NORTH
♠ 9 8 4
♡ K 3
◇ K 7 4 3 2
♣ Q 5 4

WEST
♠ A 10 6
♡ 9 8 7 6
◇ Q 5
♣ J 9 7 2

EAST
♠ 5 2
♡ A Q J 10
◇ J 10 8 6
♣ 10 8 6

SOUTH
♠ K Q J 7 3
♡ 5 4 2
◇ A 9
♣ A K 3

South is in 4♠ on the ♡8 lead. Whether South plays low or the ♡K, East wins and needs to switch to a trump. The ♠2, lowest from a doubleton, is the normal card. West must duck this, so that two more rounds of trumps can be played if South tries to ruff a heart in dummy. If West takes the ♠A at once and returns a spade, South wins and plays a heart. East wins and South cannot be prevented from ruffing a heart.

NORTH
♠ 9 7
♡ Q 9 7 4
◇ 6
♣ A Q 10 9 8 7

WEST
♠ Q 10 8 3 2
♡ K 3
◇ J 7 3 2
♣ 6 3

EAST
♠ A J 4
♡ J 10 5 2
◇ 10 9 5 4
♣ K 2

SOUTH
♠ K 6 5
♡ A 8 6
◇ A K Q 8
♣ J 5 4

West	North	East	South
			1NT
Pass	2♣	Pass	2◇
Pass	3NT	All pass	

West leads the ♠3. If East plays the instinctive ♠A and returns the ♠J, South ducks and breaks the East-West communication. East should play the ♠J at trick 1. If West's suit is headed by the K-10, this might cost a trick, but if West has Q-10-x-x-x, playing the ♠J will beat the contract, as South will not dare duck at trick 1.

NORTH
♠ K 10 6
♡ A K J 4
◇ A 10 9 5
♣ K 7

WEST
♠ J 9 7 2
♡ - - -
◇ J 8 3
♣ A 10 9 8 6 5

EAST
♠ 8 5 4
♡ Q 9 8 6 3
◇ K 7 2
♣ Q 2

SOUTH
♠ A Q 3
♡ 10 7 5 2
◇ Q 6 4
♣ J 4 3

South is in 3NT and West leads the ♣10. Let's see how Michel Lebel of France maintained communication with his partner in a match against Holland in the 1986 World Championships in Miami.

Declarer played low from dummy on the ♣10 lead and so did Lebel, East! A low heart to dummy was followed by a low diamond. East rose with the ◇K and returned the ♣Q. Two off.

Declarer could have made the contract by ducking the ♣10 lead, too, but that is feasible only if you see all four hands.

NORTH
♠ A 3
♡ A K J 6
◇ 8 6 4
♣ 10 8 6 3

WEST
♠ 10 7 6 4 2
♡ 7 4 2
◇ 5
♣ J 9 7 5

EAST
♠ K J 8
♡ Q 10 8 5
◇ A J 9 3
♣ K 2

SOUTH
♠ Q 9 5
♡ 9 3
◇ K Q 10 7 2
♣ A Q 4

Now watch Mike Lawrence, another world champion, in action.

West	North	East	South
			1◇
Pass	1♡	Pass	1NT
Pass	3NT	All pass	

West leads the ♠4, low from dummy ... Just about everyone will play the king and return the ♠J. Any chance of defeating 3NT has vanished. Lawrence, East, did not make the automatic play. Instead he played the ♠J at trick 1. Why?

Lawrence's train of thought went like this: 'On the bidding and the points in dummy and in my hand, partner can have 1-2 points at most. Partner figures to have five spades, as South did not rebid 1♠. If partner has the ♠Q, playing the ♠J cannot hurt, but if partner's spades are ten high, the ♠J must be played at trick 1.'

Double dummy, declarer can still make 3NT, but in practice the defence prevailed. South took the ♠Q, but East gained the lead twice, once to return the ♠K, unblocking, and once to play the third spade.

Sometimes it is necessary to sacrifice a trick in order to maintain communication with partner.

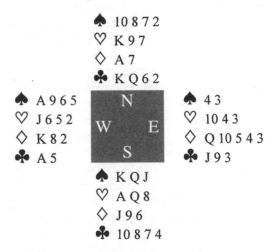

```
                    ♠  10 8 7 2
                    ♡  K 9 7
                    ◇  A 7
                    ♣  K Q 6 2
      ♠ A 9 6 5          N            ♠ 4 3
      ♡ J 6 5 2      W       E        ♡ 10 4 3
      ◇ K 8 2                         ◇ Q 10 5 4 3
      ♣ A 5              S            ♣ J 9 3
                    ♠  K Q J
                    ♡  A Q 8
                    ◇  J 9 6
                    ♣  10 8 7 4
```

South is in 3NT and West starts with a low diamond. Declarer plays low from dummy. What should East do?

If East plays the ◇Q, third-hand-high, West's inspired lead will be wasted. East should play the ◇10. This gives South two diamond tricks where there was only one, but it preserves communication between East-West and defeats the contract. Of course, West must continue the inspired play by unblocking the ◇K when in with a black ace.

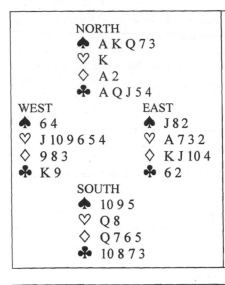

South is declarer in 6♠ after an artificial auction in which South showed 4-6 points and a balanced hand.

West leads the ♡J. Would anyone decline to capture the bare king? Marcinowi Lesniewskiemu ducked after long thought and that was the only way to beat 6♠. If East takes trick 1, South is bound to gain the lead to take the club finesse and discard the diamond loser on the ♡Q.

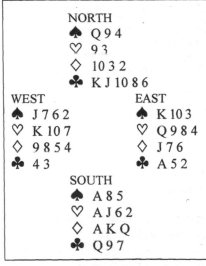

Here we return to the issue of communication, this time to destroy declarer's access to dummy.

South is in 3NT on the ♠2 lead. Declarer plays low from dummy. Which card should East play?

If East plays the ♠10, South wins and sets up the clubs. East takes the third round and switches to a low heart. South rises with the ♡A and plays a low spade to dummy's ♠9.

East-West can take two hearts, but South has an entry to dummy's clubs. Could 3NT have been defeated?

Of course. On the ♠2 lead, East should play the ♠3 to ensure that declarer cannot reach dummy via the spades later.

	NORTH		
	♠ J 10 2		
	♡ K Q J 7 4 3		
	◇ J 4		
	♣ 6 3		
WEST		EAST	
♠ Q 8 7 5 3		♠ K 9	
♡ 9 8		♡ A 6 2	
◇ A Q 3		◇ 10 9 7 6 2	
♣ 9 4 2		♣ 10 8 5	
	SOUTH		
	♠ A 6 4		
	♡ 10 5		
	◇ K 8 5		
	♣ A K Q J 7		

South is in 3NT on the ♠5 lead. Declarer plays the ♠J from dummy. What should East do?

Richard Frey, a brilliant USA player, played low and let the ♠J win. The contract now failed, but if Frey had played the ♠K at trick 1, South would set up the hearts and reach dummy via the ♠10 later.

	NORTH	
	♠ 10 9 8	
	♡ Q 7 2	
	◇ K 10 9 5	
	♣ J 9 3	
	EAST	
	♠ 6 5 3 2	
	♡ J 10 9	
	◇ A 4	
	♣ Q 8 6 4	

Here is another situation:

West	North	East	South
			2NT (1)
Pass	3NT	All pass	

(1) 20-22

West leads the ♣2, ♣3 from dummy. Is there any point in playing the queen? If West has led from the ♣K, South will still have two stoppers.

However, if West has led from ♣A-7-5-2 or similar, declarer has ♣K-x and playing the ♣Q will give declarer a second stopper in the suit. The correct card for East at trick 1 is the ♣8.

	NORTH	
	♠ 10 9 8	
	♡ Q 7 2	
	◊ K 10 9 5	
	♣ J 9 3	
WEST		EAST
♠ K 7		♠ 6 5 3 2
♡ 8 5 4 3		♡ J 10 9
◊ 7 6 2		◊ A 4
♣ A 7 5 2		♣ Q 8 6 4
	SOUTH	
	♠ A Q J 4	
	♡ A K 6	
	◊ Q J 8 3	
	♣ K 10	

Here is the complete deal. South could have made life a lot more difficult for East. With the ♣J, ♣10 and ♣9 between the two hands, it costs South nothing to play the ♣J from dummy at trick 1. This creates a real problem for East. To cover with the ♣Q is right if South began with ♣A-x, but not if South has ♣K-10. East might judge correctly, for with ♣A-x, South's normal play is the ♣9.

	NORTH	
	♠ J 8 4	
	♡ A Q 7 2	
	◊ K 9 6	
	♣ Q 7 4	
WEST		EAST
♠ Q 10 9 6 2		♠ A 7 3
♡ J 10 6 4		♡ 9 3
◊ 8		◊ 10 7 5 3 2
♣ A 10 9		♣ J 6 3
	SOUTH	
	♠ K 5	
	♡ K 8 5	
	◊ A Q J 4	
	♣ K 8 5 2	

Finally, here is an example where playing low in third seat prevents declarer from executing a squeeze against partner.

South bid 1NT and North raised to 3NT. West leads the ♠10. If East takes the ♠A and returns a spade, South will win and play four rounds of diamonds. This squeezes West. If East plays low at trick 1, there is no squeeze because East will still have an entry to the fifth diamond.

Chapter 13
Interpretation of partner's signals

These basic signals are in common use:

● In a suit played by partner, we signal attitude, with a preference for reverse attitude (low-like, high-hate).

● In a suit led by declarer, we signal count, preferably reverse count (lowest = even number, high-low = odd number).

In practice, you will find these signals alone are not adequate. Still, extra agreements can easily lead to misunderstandings. It is better to have fewer, but clear agreements than to use too complex a system, which is prone to disasters. Any additional agreements should be introduced only after the partnership is confident with the current ones.

1. The bidding can indicate the appropriate signal

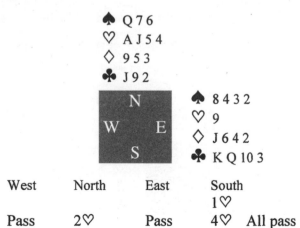

```
            ♠ Q 7 6
            ♡ A J 5 4
            ◇ 9 5 3
            ♣ J 9 2
                            ♠ 8 4 3 2
           N                ♡ 9
       W       E            ◇ J 6 4 2
           S                ♣ K Q 10 3
```

(a)	West	North	East	South
				1♡
	Pass	2♡	Pass	4♡ All pass

West leads the ♠A. Which card do you play as East?

The ♠2, encouraging a spade continuation, is out of the question. Holding ♠A-K-x-x-x, partner will assume you have a doubleton and continue spades with disastrous effect.

Suppose you have the same hand, but the auction went like this:

(b) | West | North | East | South |
|------|-------|------|-------|
| | | | 1♡ |
| 1♠ | 2♡ | 2♠ | 4♡ All pass |

Here you have promised 3+ spades and partner will take the ♠2 as showing four spades (or perhaps suit-preference for clubs).

(c) | West | North | East | South |
|------|-------|------|-------|
| | | | 1♡ |
| 1♠ | 2♡ | 3♠ | 4♡ All pass |

In this auction East has promised four spades. When dummy appears the spade position will be known. Here the ♠2 is definitely suit-preference for clubs.

If the layout of a suit is known, use a suit-preference signal.

This often applies when declarer is playing a long suit.

2. Dummy's holding can indicate the appropriate signal

```
        ♠ Q J 3
        ♡ Q J 10 9
        ◇ 9 7 5
        ♣ K 9 3
                    ♠ 9 8 5 4
                    ♡ 7 6 5
                    ◇ 8 3 2
                    ♣ A 10 2
```

South opens 1NT, North bids 2♣ (Stayman), South 2◇ and 3NT by North. West leads the ♠6, ♠Q from dummy and you play . . .?

At trick 2 declarer runs the ♡Q to West's ♡K. If you played the ♠4 at trick 1, showing an even number of spades (clearly four after the Stayman sequence), partner will continue spades.

South has:

    ♠ A 2   ♡ A 8 3   ♢ A Q J 10 6   ♣ Q 7 6

What if dummy looked like this:

    ♠ Q 3   ♡ Q J 10 9   ♢ 9 7 5 4   ♣ K 9 3

Now East should play the ♠9, discouraging and denying the ♠J. A spade continuation will give away the contract if South has:

    ♠ A J 2   ♡ A 8 3   ♢ K Q J 6   ♣ Q J 6

3. Uncovering a false card by declarer

                ♠ J 10 3
                ♡ Q 10 3
                ♢ Q J 10 8
                ♣ A 6 3

♠ Q 7 6 5 4
♡ K 5 2
♢ K 3
♣ 9 8 7

South opens 1NT and North bids 3NT. You lead the ♠5: jack – two – king. Declarer plays a club to the ace and leads ♢Q to your king. What do you play next?

Declarer's play, overtaking the ♠J with the ♠K, looks like ♠A-K doubleton. Before you rush to play another low spade to knock out the ♠A, check the cards played. If declarer did start with ♠A-K bare, partner had ♠9-8-2. Unable to beat the ♠J, partner should have played the ♠9, reverse count, but partner played the ♠2, showing an even number. What is going on?

You must trust partner and therefore South is trying to fool you into continuing spades. There is only one plausible reason. South is worried about another suit and that can only be the hearts. This is South's hand:

♠ A K 9   ♡ 9 4   ◊ A 9 6 4   ♣ K Q 5 4

After taking the ◊K, play the ♡K followed by another heart and declarer is two down. Play another spade instead and 3NT makes.

4. Recognising partner's problem

♠ 7 6 3
♡ Q 9
◊ A K J 9 3 2
♣ Q 10

♠ K 9 2
♡ J 8 5 2
◊ 10 5 4
♣ K 5 3

North opens 1◊, South 2♣, North 2◊, South 3♣, all pass. West leads the ♡3: nine – jack – king. South returns the ♡4 and partner wins with the ♡A. Which card do you play? Does it matter?

You should be wondering why partner led low away from the ♡A at trick 1. This is not a safe lead. Very limited choice is the likely reason and that suggests partner's major suits were both headed by the ace.

Put yourself in West's shoes? What information about your hand is important? The count in hearts is irrelevant. The fact that you hold the ♠K is vital. Play the ♡8 as suit-preference for spades. This is the South hand:

♠ Q 8 5   ♡ K 10 4   ◊ ---   ♣ A J 9 8 6 4 2

What if your hand looked like this:

♠ Q 9 2   ♡ J 8 5 2   ◇ 10 5 4   ♣ A 5 2

Now you should play the ♡2 at trick 2 on partner's ♡A. You want to come in with the ♣A in order to switch to the ♠Q, hoping that partner began with ♠A-J-10.

5. Who will be on lead first?

♠ A 7 2

♠ K Q 10 5 4   ♠ 9 3

♠ J 8 6

West leads the king. If declarer plays the two from dummy, East must play the nine, discouraging, to deny the jack. If declarer plays the ace, you still play the nine, discouraging, if you are not likely to come on lead. If you are confident you will be on lead before partner, you can play low if you feel the nine will mislead partner as to the distribution of the suit.

En route to deadly defence you must be aware that whichever signal you use (attitude, count, suit-preference) depends on the deal you are facing. Sometimes each partner sees the problem on the deal differently. As a result, misunderstandings occur.

The best way to reduce defensive misunderstandings is to avoid a very complex signalling system. Constant systematic partnership work will improve your defending skills. Be patient and introduce new signalling techniques later to cover specific situations. In time you and partner will be feared by every declarer.

The examples that follow illustrate defending skills at the very highest level.

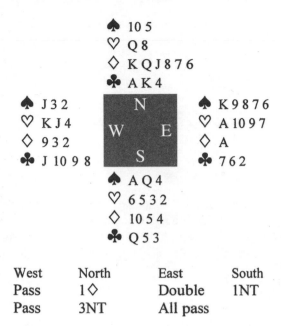

```
              ♠ 10 5
              ♥ Q 8
              ◇ K Q J 8 7 6
              ♣ A K 4
♠ J 3 2           N           ♠ K 9 8 7 6
♥ K J 4                       ♥ A 10 9 7
◇ 9 3 2      W       E        ◇ A
♣ J 10 9 8        S           ♣ 7 6 2
              ♠ A Q 4
              ♥ 6 5 3 2
              ◇ 10 5 4
              ♣ Q 5 3
```

West	North	East	South
Pass	1◇	Double	1NT
Pass	3NT	All pass	

West leads the ♣J, taken by the ace. East plays the ♣7, high-hate. Declarer continues with the ◇K and East takes it with the ◇A. Which diamond should West play?

West should recognise that this is an occasion for a suit-preference signal. Giving East count in diamonds is irrelevant because:
(a) Partner has already played the ace, not waiting for the count.
(b) Declarer has a sure entry to dummy anyway so that the number of diamonds held by West cannot be important.

Janusz Marzec, West, played the ◇2 and Roman Wojtyra, East, switched to the ♥10. West took the ♥K and assured by the lead of the *ten* of hearts, returned the ♥J to take 3NT one down.

Now try this problem:

Dealer South : North-South vulnerable

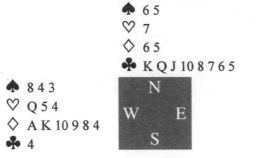

♠ 6 5
♡ 7
♢ 6 5
♣ K Q J 10 8 7 6 5

♠ 8 4 3
♡ Q 5 4
♢ A K 10 9 8 4
♣ 4

South opens 1♣, artificial, 16+ points, any shape, West bids 3♢ and North's jump to 5♣ ends the auction. The play begins:
Trick 1: ♢A: five – two – seven. Trick 2: ♢K: six – three – jack. What do you play at trick 3? After deciding, see the full deal:

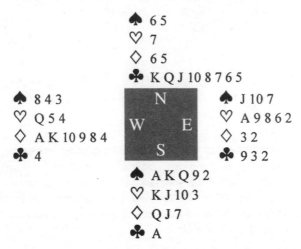

♠ 6 5
♡ 7
♢ 6 5
♣ K Q J 10 8 7 6 5

♠ 8 4 3
♡ Q 5 4
♢ A K 10 9 8 4
♣ 4

♠ J 10 7
♡ A 9 8 6 2
♢ 3 2
♣ 9 3 2

♠ A K Q 9 2
♡ K J 10 3
♢ Q J 7
♣ A

Good players know that the problem is not the distribution of the diamonds, but to find East's ace. East's carding is suit-preference, low-high in diamonds to ask for hearts, the lower suit outside clubs. With both defenders on the same wavelength, West shifts to a heart at trick 3 and the contract is defeated.

Chapter 14
Play by second hand

'Second hand low' is another rule from our grandparents' day, but is it really a good maxim to follow most of the time? What about this situation:

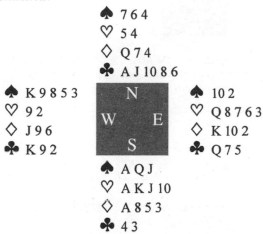

```
              ♠ 7 6 4
              ♡ 5 4
              ◇ Q 7 4
              ♣ A J 10 8 6
♠ K 9 8 5 3      N        ♠ 10 2
♡ 9 2         W     E     ♡ Q 8 7 6 3
◇ J 9 6                   ◇ K 10 2
♣ K 9 2          S        ♣ Q 7 5
              ♠ A Q J
              ♡ A K J 10
              ◇ A 8 5 3
              ♣ 4 3
```

South is in 3NT. West leads a low spade to the ten and jack. South play a low club. Which card should West play?

If West automatically plays second-hand-low, South will make 3NT easily by playing the ten or jack. If East takes the ♣Q, South can repeat the club finesse. Even if East ducks the club, South can take two heart finesses for nine tricks.

If West plays the ♣K at trick 2, the rest of the play becomes very complicated. Double dummy, South can still make 3NT by an elimination play (take the ♣A, finesse in hearts, cash the ♠A, ♡A, ♡K and exit with the last heart to endplay East), but only an expert's expert is going to find that winning line.

A psychological play to cut declarer off from dummy is the theme of this example:

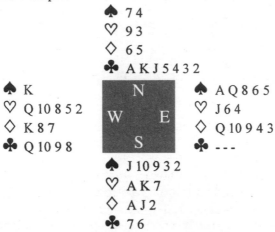

♠ 7 4
♡ 9 3
♢ 6 5
♣ A K J 5 4 3 2

♠ K
♡ Q 10 8 5 2
♢ K 8 7
♣ Q 10 9 8

♠ A Q 8 6 5
♡ J 6 4
♢ Q 10 9 4 3
♣ - - -

♠ J 10 9 3 2
♡ A K 7
♢ A J 2
♣ 7 6

South is in 3NT on a low heart lead to the jack and king. The safe route for declarer is to play a low club from both hands. When South leads a low club, what if West plays the ♣Q?

To make the contract declarer must duck the ♣Q, but how many declarers are going to do that? None at match-points and even very few at Imps, even though ducking the ♣Q guarantees 3NT.

Next, an example in no-trumps where dummy has no side entry:

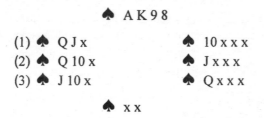

♠ A K 9 8

(1) ♠ Q J x   ♠ 10 x x x
(2) ♠ Q 10 x   ♠ J x x x
(3) ♠ J 10 x   ♠ Q x x x

♠ x x

When South leads a low spade, West has to play an honour in each case to hold declarer to two tricks. If West plays low, South can play the eight or nine and so come to three tricks.

You should play the same way if dummy had A-K-9-7 and no entry outside, since declarer might hold 8-x.

Here is a similar position:

When South leads a low card, West must play an honour if dummy has no entry. By playing high you save a trick if declarer holds two cards. That play can also be devastating if South has three low cards. You play an honour and the queen wins. When South leads low next time, you play the king. Declarer will duck this and, thinking you have K-J-10-x, might finesse on the third round. The result would be one trick for South instead of three.

Another well-known position for second-hand-high is when you need to protect partner's entry:

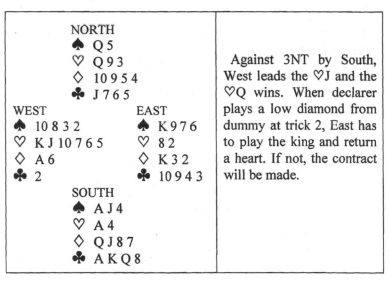

Against 3NT by South, West leads the ♡J and the ♡Q wins. When declarer plays a low diamond from dummy at trick 2, East has to play the king and return a heart. If not, the contract will be made.

```
         NORTH
      ♠ K 10 9 8 7 3
      ♡ Q 6 4
      ◇ 5 4
      ♣ 3 2
WEST              EAST
♠ - - -           ♠ 6 5
♡ A K J 10 9 8 7 5  ♡ 3 2
◇ A 9 6 3         ◇ K J 7
♣ K               ♣ 10 9 8 7 6 4
         SOUTH
      ♠ A Q J 4 2
      ♡ - - -
      ◇ Q 10 8 2
      ♣ A Q J 5
```

Here is a similar situation:

West	North	East	South
		3♣	3♠
4♡	4♠	Pass	Pass
5♡	5♠	All pass	

West's conservatism might surprise you, but East was famous for weak pre-empts. The ♡A lead is ruffed and South plays a low spade to dummy, followed by a low diamond. East has to rise with the ◇K and play a club to have any chance of defeating 5♠, else South can set up a diamond trick to pitch a club from dummy.

```
         NORTH
      ♠ 7 6 2
      ♡ A 4 3
      ◇ 10 5 4 3 2
      ♣ K 6
WEST              EAST
♠ A Q 10 3        ♠ J 8 5
♡ J 9 5           ♡ K Q 10 8 7 6
◇ J               ◇ 6
♣ J 8 7 4 3       ♣ Q 10 9
         SOUTH
      ♠ K 9 4
      ♡ 2
      ◇ A K Q 9 8 7
      ♣ A 5 2
```

Another reason to play second-hand-high is to guard against an endplay.

South is in 5◇. West leads a low heart, taken by the ace. South ruffs a heart, draws trumps, club to the king, heart ruff, ♣A, club ruff, followed by a low spade from dummy. If East plays low, South inserts the ♠9 and West is endplayed. If East plays the ♠J on the first spade, the contract will be defeated.

Now let's see Paul Hackett (W) and Martin Hoffman (E) on defence:

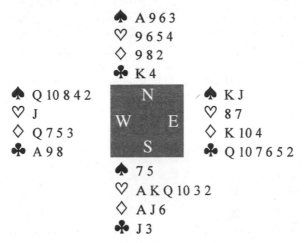

♠ A 9 6 3
♡ 9 6 5 4
◇ 9 8 2
♣ K 4

♠ Q 10 8 4 2   ♠ K J
♡ J   ♡ 8 7
◇ Q 7 5 3   ◇ K 10 4
♣ A 9 8   ♣ Q 10 7 6 5 2

♠ 7 5
♡ A K Q 10 3 2
◇ A J 6
♣ J 3

West led the ♠4 against 4♡. South ducked in dummy, won the next spade and ruffed a spade with the ♡10. After the ♡A, ♡K, South played a low club. West took the ♣A and exited with a club. Declarer ruffed another spade and crossed to dummy with a heart. This was the position:

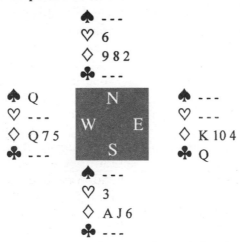

♠ - - -
♡ 6
◇ 9 8 2
♣ - - -

♠ Q   ♠ - - -
♡ - - -   ♡ - - -
◇ Q 7 5   ◇ K 10 4
♣ - - -   ♣ Q

♠ - - -
♡ 3
◇ A J 6
♣ - - -

When the ♢9 was led from dummy, Hoffman played the ♢K, the only certain way to defeat the contract. Had he played second-hand-low, declarer also plays low and West is endplayed.

This layout requires a similar defence against a throw-in play:

♠ K 8 2

♠ A Q 4 3   ♠ 9 7 5

♠ J 10 6

Sometimes second-hand-high does not seem to damage declarer, but you never can tell. Witness this deal from the semi-finals of the 1984 World Championships:

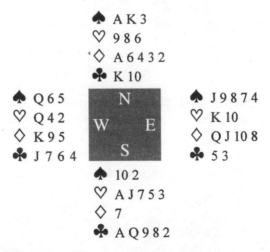

♠ A K 3
♡ 9 8 6
♢ A 6 4 3 2
♣ K 10

♠ Q 6 5   N   ♠ J 9 8 7 4
♡ Q 4 2   W   E   ♡ K 10
♢ K 9 5   ♢ Q J 10 8
♣ J 7 6 4   S   ♣ 5 3

♠ 10 2
♡ A J 7 5 3
♢ 7
♣ A Q 9 8 2

Each table bid to 6♡, which seems to have no problems. Win the spade lead, finesse the ♡J, win any return, cash the ♡A, ruff the third club and claim. In practice, all four Easts (De Falco, Lebel, Weichsel and Wold) played the ♡K on the low heart from dummy at trick 2. This apparently innocuous play complicated declarer's play considerably. Two declarers (Cronier and Hamman) returned to dummy with a club and played another heart.

West won and played a third heart. One down. The other two declarers (Belladonna and Passell) tried to ruff the third round of clubs, but East over-ruffed with the ♡10. One down.

Playing an honour second-hand-high may also lure declarer into a losing line. Witness this deal from the 1986 Polish National Trials:

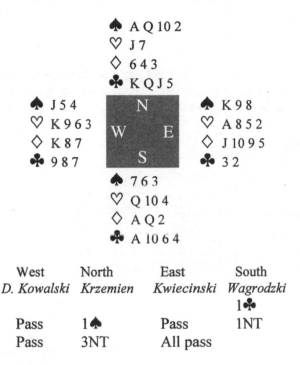

```
              ♠ A Q 10 2
              ♡ J 7
              ◇ 6 4 3
              ♣ K Q J 5
♠ J 5 4                        ♠ K 9 8
♡ K 9 6 3        N             ♡ A 8 5 2
◇ K 8 7       W     E          ◇ J 10 9 5
♣ 9 8 7          S             ♣ 3 2
              ♠ 7 6 3
              ♡ Q 10 4
              ◇ A Q 2
              ♣ A 10 6 4
```

West	North	East	South
D. Kowalski	Krzemien	Kwiecinski	Wagrodzki
			1♣
Pass	1♠	Pass	1NT
Pass	3NT	All pass	

The ♡3 lead went to the ace and on the ♡2 return, West let the ♡Q win. South played a low spade: jack – queen – king. East shifted to a low diamond. South had a problem: was the diamond finesse working or were spades 3-3? Taken in by West's play of the ♠J, South assumed it was from J-x (who plays the jack in second seat from jack third?). South went for the diamond finesse. One down.

NORTH
♠ A J 10 9 8
♡ A 7 3 2
◇ 5 2
♣ 8 2

WEST
♠ K 2
♡ Q J 5
◇ 10 9 7 6
♣ J 10 7 3

EAST
♠ Q 7 6 3
♡ K 10 9 8 4
◇ 3
♣ A 9 6

SOUTH
♠ 5 4
♡ 6
◇ A K Q J 8 4
♣ K Q 5 4

The defenders on this deal from a Masters Tournament in Deauville were Omar Sharif and Claude Delmouly.

West led the ♡Q against South's 5◇. Declarer took the ace and played a club to the king, followed by a low spade. Sharif rose with the ♠K, taken by the ace. On the next club Delmouly played the ace, cashed the ♠Q and led a third spade, thus promoting a trump trick for West.

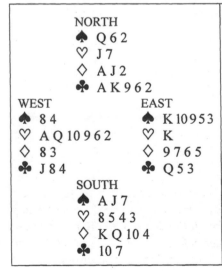

NORTH
♠ Q 6 2
♡ J 7
◇ A J 2
♣ A K 9 6 2

WEST
♠ 8 4
♡ A Q 10 9 6 2
◇ 8 3
♣ J 8 4

EAST
♠ K 10 9 5 3
♡ K
◇ 9 7 6 5
♣ Q 5 3

SOUTH
♠ A J 7
♡ 8 5 4 3
◇ K Q 10 4
♣ 10 7

Finally, a deal which has become a bridge classic.

West	North	East	South
Sheinwold	*Sobel*	*Jacoby*	*Goren*
	1♣	2♠	2NT
3♡	3NT	All pass	

West led a low spade. Goren won with the ♠J and judged that West's failure to lead a heart meant that he was missing an honour, probably the king. To sever the connection between East and West, Goren played a heart from hand at trick 2.

Had West played low or the ♡Q, South could succeed, but West read South's plan and rose with the ♡A to beat 3NT by two tricks.

Chapter 15
Confirming the opening lead

Dorothy Hayden Truscott, the brilliant American, proposed an idea for defence against no-trumps. Her 'tip' received the highest mark awarded by the International Bridge Press Association. Consider:

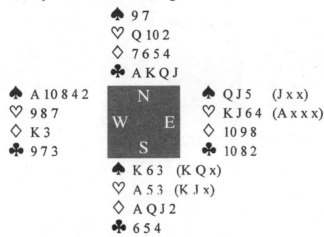

```
              ♠ 97
              ♡ Q 10 2
              ◇ 7 6 5 4
              ♣ A K Q J
♠ A 10 8 4 2                  ♠ Q J 5   (J x x)
♡ 9 8 7        N              ♡ K J 6 4 (A x x x)
◇ K 3      W       E          ◇ 10 9 8
♣ 9 7 3        S              ♣ 10 8 2
              ♠ K 6 3   (K Q x)
              ♡ A 5 3   (K J x)
              ◇ A Q J 2
              ♣ 6 5 4
```

North opens 1♣ and South's 3NT response is passed out. West leads the ♠4. South captures East's jack, crosses to dummy with a club and takes the diamond finesse, losing to West.

With the layout above, West should continue spades, but if the position is as in parentheses, West needs to shift to hearts for East to win and return a spade. East is the one who needs to let partner know which path to take: *When following suit to the first suit led by declarer, a low card by either defender is an encouraging signal, asking partner to continue the suit led; high is discouraging.*

On this deal, with ♠Q-J-x, East plays the ♣2 on the second trick; with the ♠J-x-x holding, East should follow with the ♣10.

This signal is also known as Reverse Smith Echo. The original Smith Echo was to follow with a high card if you liked the suit led, lowest if you did not. The Hayden approach, 'reverse Smith', is more economical when you like the suit led.

The signal can also be used by the opening leader. For example:

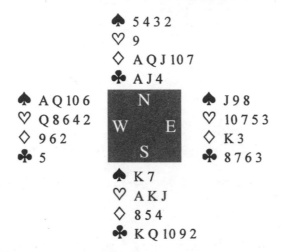

```
                    ♠ 5 4 3 2
                    ♡ 9
                    ◇ A Q J 10 7
                    ♣ A J 4
   ♠ A Q 10 6          N          ♠ J 9 8
   ♡ Q 8 6 4 2      W     E       ♡ 10 7 5 3
   ◇ 9 6 2                         ◇ K 3
   ♣ 5                 S          ♣ 8 7 6 3
                    ♠ K 7
                    ♡ A K J
                    ◇ 8 5 4
                    ♣ K Q 10 9 2
```

West leads the ♡4 against South's 3NT. South takes East's ♡10 and finesses the ◇Q, losing to East. On this trick, West followed with the ◇9 to signal no interest in a heart return. East switches to a spade and 3NT is defeated. In some layouts, such as ♠J-x-x with East, ♠x-x-x in dummy and ♠K-9-x with South, East will need to shift to the ♠J to collect four spade tricks for the defence.

The Hayden confirmation/denial of opening lead signal is just as valuable as encourage/discourage signals on partner's lead. You should treat it as mandatory. Here is a deal from the Polish First Division Competition:

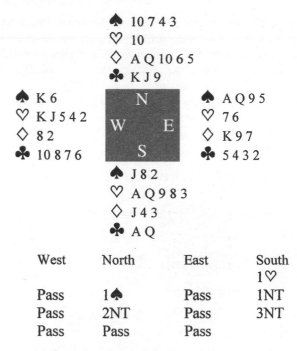

West	North	East	South
			1♡
Pass	1♠	Pass	1NT
Pass	2NT	Pass	3NT
Pass	Pass	Pass	

West began with the ♣8: nine – five – ace. South ran the ◇J, ducked by East, and repeated the diamond finesse, losing to the king. It is very tempting for East to switch to spades, in case the layout looks like this:

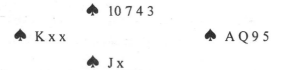

Here East needs to play top spade, followed by the ♠5. That is in fact what East did on the actual deal and, as you can see, 3NT now succeeds. To prevent East from going wrong, West should play ◇2, then ◇8, requesting a continuation of clubs. With those hearts over declarer, West knows the spade shift is not urgent.

Denying interest in the suit led does not necessarily deny values in that suit, but rather it is a suggestion to change the thrust of the defence. Showing interest in the suit led says, 'Partner, no need to do anything special,' while discouraging the suit led shows a desire for a switch to some other suit.

In practice, Dorothy Hayden's signal has proved very useful and is therefore used by many top pairs. On the next deal, the defenders were not using this signal and failed to defeat 3NT.

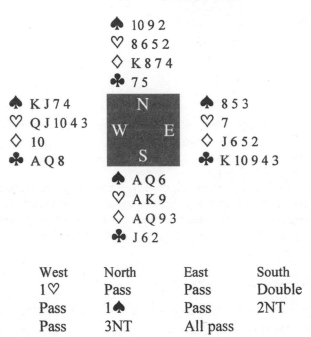

	♠ 10 9 2	
	♡ 8 6 5 2	
	◇ K 8 7 4	
	♣ 7 5	

♠ K J 7 4   ♠ 8 5 3
♡ Q J 10 4 3   ♡ 7
◇ 10   ◇ J 6 5 2
♣ A Q 8   ♣ K 10 9 4 3

♠ A Q 6
♡ A K 9
◇ A Q 9 3
♣ J 6 2

West	North	East	South
1♡	Pass	Pass	Double
Pass	1♠	Pass	2NT
Pass	3NT	All pass	

West led the ♡Q. South won with the ace and played the ◇A, then the ◇9 to the king, followed by the ◇8, which won. West discarded a low spade and a low club. At trick 5, declarer ran the ♠10 to West's jack. Hoping South had started with ♡A-K bare, West played the ♡3. South won with the ♡9 and cashed the ♡K.

These cards remained:

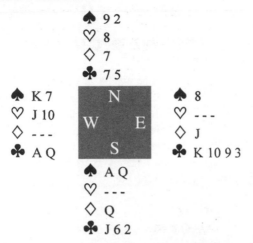

When South cashed the ◇Q, West, annoyed with himself, threw the ♣A. Now South led the ♣2 and had to come to a ninth trick either via the ♠A-Q or the ♣J, if East overtakes the ♣Q.

The contract is easy to defeat, especially if East uses the Hayden signal (◇6 on the ◇A to deny interest in hearts), followed by a suit-preference signal (◇2, then ◇5, to show interest in clubs). Even at the end 3NT can be defeated if West throws a heart winner on the ◇Q.

Some useful lessons can be drawn from this deal:

● Never give up, even if the early defence was unsuccessful and the position seems to be hopeless.

● Strive constantly to improve your defensive methods. Adopting the Hayden signal, 'confirmation/denial of the suit led', would have helped East-West greatly here.

● Take every opportunity possible to signal as much information to partner as you can by using suit-preference and count signals.

Chapter 16
First to play

Is there a problem? After all, there are basic rules: fourth-highest from your longest and strongest, low from three to an honour, top from a doubleton, etc. These rules apply only to the opening lead. After dummy appears, these rules often change. The examples in Chapter 5 *Surround Plays* illustrated some quite non-standard leads late in the play. Sometimes, even as early as trick 1, good judgment indicates the need for a non-standard lead:

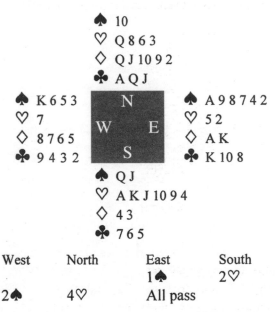

	♠ 10		
	♡ Q 8 6 3		
	♢ Q J 10 9 2		
	♣ A Q J		

♠ K 6 5 3		♠ A 9 8 7 4 2
♡ 7	N	♡ 5 2
♢ 8 7 6 5	W E	♢ A K
♣ 9 4 3 2	S	♣ K 10 8

	♠ Q J
	♡ A K J 10 9 4
	♢ 4 3
	♣ 7 6 5

West	North	East	South
		1♠	2♡
2♠	4♡	All pass	

The normal lead of a low spade allows 4♡ to make. Declarer will establish diamonds and discard losing clubs. Is that East's fault, because he did not bid 4♠, which is cold? Yes, that's true, but that is no reason to allow South to make 4♡.

Lacking entries, West should lead the ♠K. Winning the trick, West can see the need to play a club through dummy. One down.

Dealer North : North-South vulnerable

West	North	East	South
	Pass	1♠	4♡
4♠	Pass	Pass	Dble
Pass	5♡	All pass	

What would you lead as West with:

♠ J 8 2   ♡ 2   ◇ A Q 9 3 2   ♣ 9 8 5 2

The deal arose in a national teams championship in 2009:

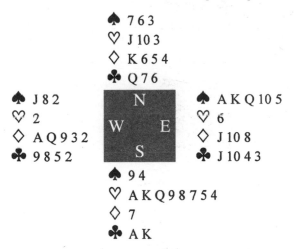

```
              ♠ 7 6 3
              ♡ J 10 3
              ◇ K 6 5 4
              ♣ Q 7 6
♠ J 8 2          N          ♠ A K Q 10 5
♡ 2                         ♡ 6
◇ A Q 9 3 2   W      E      ◇ J 10 8
♣ 9 8 5 2        S          ♣ J 10 4 3
              ♠ 9 4
              ♡ A K Q 9 8 7 5 4
              ◇ 7
              ♣ A K
```

At some tables West led the ♠2. East won with the ♠Q and switched to the ◇J. West took the ◇A and returned a diamond and so 5♡ made. This was poor. With six spades, East would have won trick 1 with the ♠A to ensure no spade continuation. Ron Klinger, Australia, made life easier for the defence by leading the ♣J. East played the ♠10, reverse count, and so West cashed the ◇A, followed by another spade. An easy one down.

Leading an unsupported honour is also a good idea if the bidding indicates that dummy has an honour in the suit. For example:

West	North	East	South
		1♡	1♠
Pass	1NT	Pass	2♣
Pass	3♠	All pass	

After this auction, if you have ♡Q-x-x, you should lead the queen to play through and possibly trap dummy's ♡K-x-x.

There is another reason to lead an honour if declarer is expected to hold a shortage in this suit. By leading an honour we might be able to pin a singleton queen or jack or perhaps a doubleton ten.

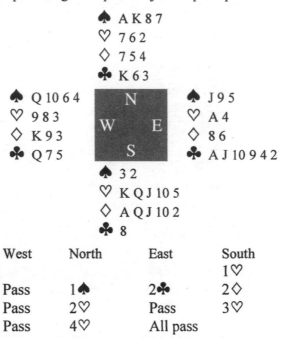

```
              ♠ A K 8 7
              ♡ 7 6 2
              ◇ 7 5 4
              ♣ K 6 3
  ♠ Q 10 6 4      N       ♠ J 9 5
  ♡ 9 8 3                 ♡ A 4
  ◇ K 9 3     W     E     ◇ 8 6
  ♣ Q 7 5                 ♣ A J 10 9 4 2
                  S
              ♠ 3 2
              ♡ K Q J 10 5
              ◇ A Q J 10 2
              ♣ 8
```

West	North	East	South
			1♡
Pass	1♠	2♣	2◇
Pass	2♡	Pass	3♡
Pass	4♡	All pass	

After the normal lead of a low club, 4♡ is unbeatable. However, Terence Reese led the ♣Q and that changed the outcome.

When declarer ducked in dummy, West led a second club. East won and the third club shortened declarer. Declarer started on the trumps and on taking the ♡A, East played a fourth club. South ruffed high and drew trumps. A spade to dummy was followed by the diamond finesse. Reese naturally ducked. South returned to dummy with a spade and repeated the diamond finesse. West won and East took the rest of the tricks with the ♠J and the clubs for three off.

Here is another example, already a classical case, from the final of the 1987 Bermuda Bowl:

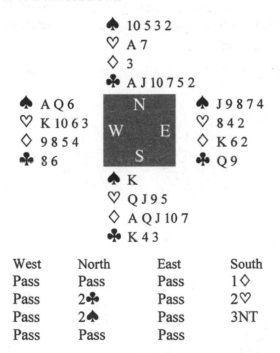

```
              ♠ 10 5 3 2
              ♡ A 7
              ◇ 3
              ♣ A J 10 7 5 2
  ♠ A Q 6        N        ♠ J 9 8 7 4
  ♡ K 10 6 3              ♡ 8 4 2
  ◇ 9 8 5 4   W     E     ◇ K 6 2
  ♣ 8 6          S        ♣ Q 9
              ♠ K
              ♡ Q J 9 5
              ◇ A Q J 10 7
              ♣ K 4 3
```

West	North	East	South
Pass	Pass	Pass	1◇
Pass	2♣	Pass	2♡
Pass	2♠	Pass	3NT
Pass	Pass	Pass	

Franco led the ♠A and, capturing the singleton king, defeated 3NT forthwith, but such deals and such leads seldom happen, unlike the non-standard leads later in the play.

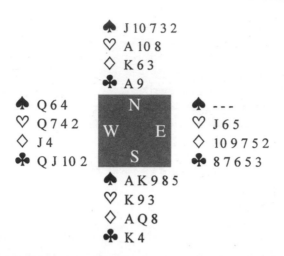

♠ J 10 7 3 2
♡ A 10 8
◇ K 6 3
♣ A 9

♠ Q 6 4
♡ Q 7 4 2
◇ J 4
♣ Q J 10 2

♠ - - -
♡ J 6 5
◇ 10 9 7 5 2
♣ 8 7 6 5 3

♠ A K 9 8 5
♡ K 9 3
◇ A Q 8
♣ K 4

Against 6♠ by South, West led the ♣Q. South won, drew two rounds of trumps, eliminated the clubs and diamonds and endplayed West with the third spade.

Clearly West must lead a heart, but which one? If West plays a low heart, declarer ducks in dummy and East plays the jack. South takes it and continues with a finesse of the ♡10 to land the slam.

Suppose West switches to the ♡Q instead of a low one. How will that alter things?

West has now given declarer a choice. Does West have both queen and jack (win with the ♡K and finesse the ♡10) or is the ♡Q lead top from worthless cards (take the ♡A and finesse the ♡9).

The Rule of Restricted Choice might lead declarer to adopt the second line, but does declarer always do the right thing? In any event, by leading the ♡Q West has created a significant losing option, which would not exist after a switch to a low heart.

By changing just one card in the above diagram, the situation is changed dramatically:

```
              NORTH
          ♠ J 10 7 3 2
          ♡ A 10 8
          ◇ K 6 3
          ♣ A 9
WEST                    EAST
♠ Q 6 4                 ♠ - - -
♡ Q 9 4 2               ♡ J 6 5
◇ J 4                   ◇ 10 9 7 5 2
♣ Q J 10 2              ♣ 8 7 6 5 3
              SOUTH
          ♠ A K 9 8 5
          ♡ K 7 3
          ◇ A Q 8
          ♣ K 4
```

The ♡9 and the ♡7 have been swapped in the South and West hands. Now after the same start to the play, the ♡Q shift always beats the slam.

```
              NORTH
          ♠ A Q 5 4
          ♡ 9 5 4
          ◇ 5
          ♣ A K Q 10 8
WEST                    EAST
♠ 6                     ♠ 8 7
♡ A J 10                ♡ Q 8 6 3
◇ J 10 9 7 4            ◇ A 8 3 2
♣ J 4 3 2               ♣ 9 7 6
              SOUTH
          ♠ K J 10 9 3 2
          ♡ K 7 2
          ◇ K Q 6
          ♣ 5
```

West	North	East	South
			1♠
Pass	2♣	Pass	2♠
Pass	4◇	Pass	4♠
Pass	Pass	Pass	

West starts with the ◇J to East's ace. What next?

With no tricks from the black suits, we need three heart tricks. The only hope is to find ♡A-J-10 with West. (Not ♡A-K-x – West would have led that.) East has to shift to a heart, but it must be the ♡Q. If South ducks that, the next heart will defeat the contract.

Note that the tactics for choosing which card to lead can change according to the level of the contract. If South was in 5♠ on the preceding deal, should East still lead the ♡Q? Of course not. Now all that is needed to defeat the contract are two heart tricks. It will be enough if West has ♡A-J. A low heart might do if West has the ♡A and South misguesses with ♡K-J. If you lead the ♡Q, South cannot misguess.

Let's interchange the ♡9 and the ♡10:

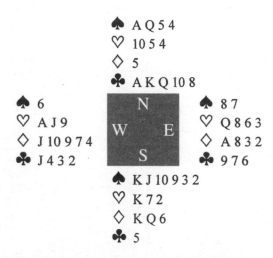

```
               ♠ A Q 5 4
               ♡ 10 5 4
               ◇ 5
               ♣ A K Q 10 8
   ♠ 6                          ♠ 8 7
   ♡ A J 9          N           ♡ Q 8 6 3
   ◇ J 10 9 7 4   W   E         ◇ A 8 3 2
   ♣ J 4 3 2        S           ♣ 9 7 6
               ♠ K J 10 9 3 2
               ♡ K 7 2
               ◇ K Q 6
               ♣ 5
```

South is in 4♠ and it seems that the defence has no hope. After the ◇J lead to the ◇A and the ♡Q switch, South can cover with the king and the ♡10 will stop the defence collecting a third heart trick.

Will South definitely cover the ♡Q with the ♡K? Perhaps South will play East to hold ♡Q-J. If so, South has to duck the ♡Q to avoid losing three tricks. That is exactly what East hopes will happen. If South ducks the ♡Q, East plays another heart and the defence comes out on top.

Let's look at what happens by changing just one card again:

NORTH
♠ A Q 5 4
♡ 10 5 4
♢ 5
♣ A K Q 10 8

WEST
♠ 6
♡ J 9 6
♢ J 10 9 7 4
♣ J 4 3 2

EAST
♠ 8 7
♡ A Q 8 3
♢ A 8 3 2
♣ 9 7 6

SOUTH
♠ K J 10 9 3 2
♡ K 7 2
♢ K Q 6
♣ 5

Now the situation looks to be totally hopeless for the defence, but only if South can see all four hands. What if East wins trick 1 with the ♢A and again shifts to the ♡Q? If South plays East for ♡Q-J and ducks the ♡Q, East should continue with a low heart. Would South now play the ♡K? One cannot be sure. It all depends on the expertise of declarer and how highly he rates the opponents' skill.

NORTH
♠ A 8 4 3
♡ 10 8 7
♢ A Q 9 6
♣ K 8

WEST
♠ 10 9 7
♡ A J 5 3
♢ K 8 7 3
♣ Q 7

EAST
♠ K J 6
♡ Q 9 4
♢ 5 4 2
♣ 10 9 3 2

SOUTH
♠ Q 5 2
♡ K 6 2
♢ J 10
♣ A J 6 5 4

Here is an example how they play in the Bermuda Bowl. This arose in a final between Italy and the USA. At both tables South was in 2♣ on the ♠10 lead, low from dummy. Both East players (Garozzo and Goldman) took the ♠K and switched to the ♡Q: king – ace. West returned the ♡3 and both declarers (Wolff and Bianchi) played the same way. They made the winning move by rising with the ten.

Here is another way to play on declarer's nerves and possibly succeed via a deceptive play:

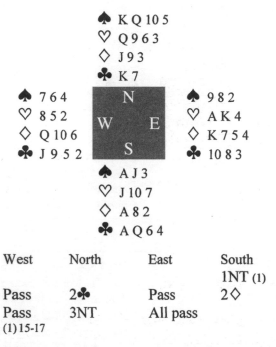

♠ K Q 10 5
♡ Q 9 6 3
◇ J 9 3
♣ K 7

♠ 7 6 4   ♠ 9 8 2
♡ 8 5 2   ♡ A K 4
◇ Q 10 6   ◇ K 7 5 4
♣ J 9 5 2   ♣ 10 8 3

♠ A J 3
♡ J 10 7
◇ A 8 2
♣ A Q 6 4

West	North	East	South
			1NT (1)
Pass	2♣	Pass	2◇
Pass	3NT	All pass	
(1) 15-17			

West leads the ♣2: seven – ten – queen. South plays the ♡J, won by your king. How should you continue?

With the points revealed West cannot have much. You can place South with the ♣A (with ♣Q-x-x-x, he would have played the ♣K from dummy). The best hope is find West with ◇Q and ◇10, but a switch to a low diamond will not do. South can duck and insert the ◇9 from dummy on the diamond return.

How about trying the ◇K? Afraid that this lead could be from ◇K-Q-10-x and that West has the ♡A, South might duck. If he also ducks the next diamond, the defenders can set up a fifth trick.

Here is a similar play by Levit of Israel:

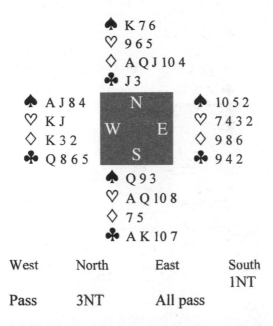

| ♠ K 7 6 |
| ♡ 9 6 5 |
| ◇ A Q J 10 4 |
| ♣ J 3 |

♠ A J 8 4	♠ 10 5 2
♡ K J	♡ 7 4 3 2
◇ K 3 2	◇ 9 8 6
♣ Q 8 6 5	♣ 9 4 2

| ♠ Q 9 3 |
| ♡ A Q 10 8 |
| ◇ 7 5 |
| ♣ A K 10 7 |

West	North	East	South
			1NT
Pass	3NT	All pass	

West began with a low club, taken by dummy's jack. South ran the ♡9, losing to the jack. Levit made the obvious switch to a spade, but he did not lead a low spade, as many might have done. Instead he played the jack of spades. This ran to South's queen and after finessing in diamonds, declarer played a heart from dummy to his queen and West's king.

Now Levit's early manoeuvre paid off when he continued with a low spade. South, convinced that West had started with ♠J-10, played low from dummy. East won with the ♠10 and returned a spade to West's ace. The thirteenth spade gave the defenders their fifth trick.

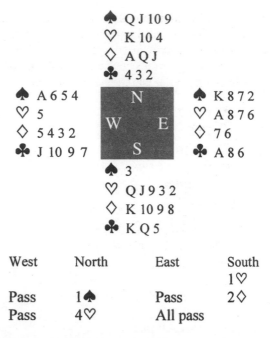

♠ Q J 10 9
♡ K 10 4
◇ A Q J
♣ 4 3 2

♠ A 6 5 4
♡ 5
◇ 5 4 3 2
♣ J 10 9 7

♠ K 8 7 2
♡ A 8 7 6
◇ 7 6
♣ A 8 6

♠ 3
♡ Q J 9 3 2
◇ K 10 9 8
♣ K Q 5

West	North	East	South
			1♡
Pass	1♠	Pass	2◇
Pass	4♡	All pass	

West leads the ♣J: two – ace – five. You know South has at least nine cards in the red suits. If he also started with ♣K-Q-5, he will have at most one spade. If it is the ♠A, the contract is unbeatable. Therefore you must assume that partner has the ♠A and your task is to shorten declarer's trumps.

Playing a low spade will not work. That would shorten declarer only once, because then dummy's spades will be high. You have to switch to the ♠K, followed by a low spade. If declarer discards on the second spade, you have four tricks. If declarer ruffs, you will play another spade when you come in with the ♡A.

If South discards, West wins and if South ruffs the third spade, you have trump control and will take an extra trick in trumps later.

We now come to some card combinations where it is essential to lead an honour. You will do well to memorize them so that you can recognize them easily when they arise at the table. Here is a deal from the Rotterdam Bridge Marathon, where the defenders were Schwartz and Birman from the Israeli national team:

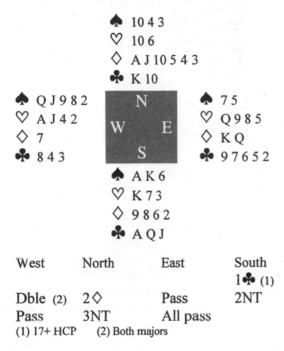

```
                    ♠ 10 4 3
                    ♡ 10 6
                    ◇ A J 10 5 4 3
                    ♣ K 10
      ♠ Q J 9 8 2         N          ♠ 7 5
      ♡ A J 4 2      W         E      ♡ Q 9 8 5
      ◇ 7                 S          ◇ K Q
      ♣ 8 4 3                        ♣ 9 7 6 5 2
                    ♠ A K 6
                    ♡ K 7 3
                    ◇ 9 8 6 2
                    ♣ A Q J
```

West	North	East	South
			1♣ (1)
Dble (2)	2◇	Pass	2NT
Pass	3NT	All pass	

(1) 17+ HCP   (2) Both majors

West began with the ♠Q, won by the king. South played a diamond to the ace and another diamond. David Birman won and analysed the situation after West discarded the ♣3. 'West's spades will not be headed by the A-Q-J, else he would have discarded a higher club. Also declarer must be afraid of something because he did not safety play the diamonds (finessing in case West had started with ◇K-Q-7). South does not want me to come on lead and so his fear must be the heart suit. In that case, here comes the ♡Q.' It was the only card to defeat the contract.

NORTH
♠ A 10
♡ J 8 7 4
◇ K 3
♣ J 10 8 7 6

WEST
♠ 8 7 3 2
♡ K 5 2
◇ Q J 10 7 6
♣ 2

EAST
♠ 6 5 4
♡ A Q 9 3
◇ 8 5 2
♣ A 5 3

SOUTH
♠ K Q J 9
♡ 10 6
◇ A 9 4
♣ K Q 9 4

West	North	East	South
			1NT
Pass	2♣	Pass	2♠
Pass	3NT	All pass	

West leads the ◇Q, taken by the ◇A. South plays the ♣K, followed by the ♣Q. East wins and can see that the only hope is for four tricks from the hearts. That is only possible if West has K-x-x. You cannot afford to play a low heart. That requires West to have the ♡10 as well. Play the ♡A or the ♡Q, followed by a low heart and all is well.

NORTH
♠ J 5
♡ Q 7
◇ Q J 10 9 6 3
♣ A 10 9

WEST
♠ Q 10 8 7 2
♡ K J 9 4
◇ A 4
♣ 9 2

EAST
♠ 9 4 3
♡ A 3 2
◇ 8 7 2
♣ 7 6 4 3

SOUTH
♠ A K 6
♡ 10 8 6 5
◇ K 5
♣ K Q J 5

West	North	East	South
			1NT
Pass	3NT	All pass	

West leads the ♠7 and the ♠J wins trick 1. South plays a low diamond to the king and ace. West can see that South has nine tricks via three spades, five diamonds and the ♣A. Four heart tricks are needed urgently. Again a low card does not work. West must lead the ♡K, then a low heart to the ace and a heart from East.

South might have made it harder for the defence by overtaking the
♠J with the ♠K at trick 1. He had plenty of winners and did not
need an extra trick from the spades. The upshot would be that West
could not have counted nine sure tricks for South and might have
continued with a second spade.

Leading the king first would also be essential if the layout of the
heart suit had been like this:

♡ Q 7

♡ K J 8 4   ♡ A 9 2

♡ 10 6 5 3

Of course, East has to unblock the nine under the king, even
though that might appear to be a discouraging signal. When the
♡K wins, West will realize the situation. If East plays the ♡2 on
the king and wins the ♡A next, the ♡9 will follow. South can
now succeed by playing low. The ♡9 blocks the suit and West
cannot afford to overtake.

This position is similar and now West needs to unblock the nine:

♡ J 5 4 3

♡ A 9 7   ♡ K Q 8 2

♡ 10 6

Playing the ♡A first will not allow you to take four heart tricks
immediately. It has to be a low heart, but if West starts with the
♡7, East wins with the ♡Q and returns the ♡2. The trouble is
that the ♡9 now blocks the suit if South ducks in dummy.

To take four tricks quickly, West has to lead the nine, even though
this looks like a discouraging, high-hate lead. East wins with the
♡Q and returns the ♡2. Now the ♡7 allows East to take two
more tricks.

NORTH
♠ K J 9 5
♡ J 6 5 4
◇ A 3
♣ Q J 10

WEST
♠ A 10 6 4
♡ A 9 3
◇ 10 8 2
♣ K 7 5

EAST
♠ 8 2
♡ K Q 8 2
◇ 9 6 5
♣ 9 6 4 3

SOUTH
♠ Q 7 3
♡ 10 7
◇ K Q J 7 4
♣ A 8 2

Claude Blouquil, a French international, put this lesson into practice on this deal.

West	North	East	South
			1◇
Pass	1♡	Pass	1NT
Pass	3NT	All pass	

West led ♠4 and dummy's ♠9 won the trick. Declarer ran the ♣Q to West's ♣K. Blouquil produced the right continuation, the ♡9, and declarer was soon one off.

NORTH
♠ A K 10
♡ 6
◇ K J 9 8 5
♣ Q 7 4 2

WEST
♠ Q 2
♡ 10 7 4 3 2
◇ 6 4 3
♣ 8 6 5

EAST
♠ J 9 7 6 5 4
♡ A J 9
◇ A Q
♣ 10 3

SOUTH
♠ 8 3
♡ K Q 8 5
◇ 10 7 2
♣ A K J 9

Now let's see Rixi Markus in action:

West	North	East	South
			1NT
Pass	2♣	2♠	Pass
Pass	Dble	Pass	3♡
Pass	3NT	All pass	

The standard lead of the ♠Q, top from a doubleton, will not work. When in with a diamond, East cannot continue the spades without costing a trick. Rixi's reasoning: 'South removed North's penalty double and so will not have much in spades. As I have no entry, I will start with the ♠2.'

After this lead, declarer was helpless. He took the ♠A, came to hand with a club and ran the ◇7. East won with the ◇Q and returned a spade. Declarer ducked the queen, but Rixi put East in with the ♡A. The next spade set up East's remaining spades and declarer could not come to more than eight tricks.

Another situation where it might be best to lead low from honour doubleton occurs when declarer is playing no-trumps and partner has shown a long, good suit, but possibly with no outside entry.

♣ 3

♣ K 5   ♣ A J 10 8 7 4 2

♣ Q 9 6

Imagine East has pre-empted in clubs and South is in 3NT. If we start off with the ♣K, we can never collect more than two club tricks if East has no side entry.

What if West leads the ♣5? If East plays the ♣10 and South takes the ♣Q, then if we gain the lead and play the ♣K, East can overtake and we take six tricks. Of course, South can duck East's ♣10, but that would look foolish if East had ♣A-K-J-10-8-7-4.

Here is a similar case:

◇ 2

◇ Q 4   ◇ A K 10 9 7 6

◇ J 8 5 3

East pre-empted in diamonds and South is in 3NT. If West leads the ◇Q and another diamond, the defence can take only three diamond tricks if East is without an entry. The lead of the ◇4 allows East to play the ◇9 (playing South for ◇Q-x-x, West for ◇J-x-x). If South takes the ◇J and West gains the lead later, the ◇Q is overtaken by East and the defence can collect five diamond tricks.

Here is Rixi Markus again, this time in partnership with the famous Benito Garozzo:

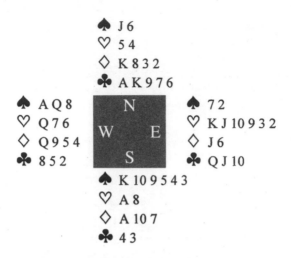

```
              ♠ J 6
              ♡ 5 4
              ◇ K 8 3 2
              ♣ A K 9 7 6
  ♠ A Q 8        N         ♠ 7 2
  ♡ Q 7 6                  ♡ K J 10 9 3 2
  ◇ Q 9 5 4   W     E      ◇ J 6
  ♣ 8 5 2        S         ♣ Q J 10
              ♠ K 10 9 5 4 3
              ♡ A 8
              ◇ A 10 7
              ♣ 4 3
```

After a 3♡ opening by Markus, East, South became declarer in 4♠. Garozzo, West, led the ♡Q and East overtook with the ♡K. South won with the ace, crossed to dummy in clubs and took the spade finesse. West won with the ♠Q and played a second heart, taken by East. How should East continue?

With the threat of dummy's clubs becoming established, it is imperative to switch to diamonds, either to create a trick there or to remove the entry to dummy before the clubs are set up. Again, it will not work if East starts with the ◇J. South can win with the ◇A and West, when in with the ace of trumps, will not be able to continue diamonds without giving away a trick. Markus shifted to the essential ◇6 and the contract was defeated.